PENGUIN BOOKS

THE CLASSIC TEN

Nancy MacDonell Smith is the fashion news/features director at *NYLON* magazine. She has written about fashion and style for *The New York Times, Harper's Bazaar, Wallpaper,* and *New York* magazine. She was born in Montreal and now lives in New York City. *The Classic Ten* is her first book.

The Classic Ten

THE TRUE STORY OF
THE LITTLE BLACK DRESS
AND NINE OTHER
FASHION FAVORITES

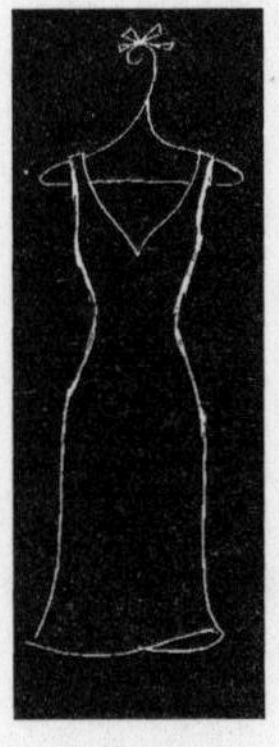

Nancy
MacDonell
Smith

Penguin Books

PENGUIN BOOKS

Published by the Penguin Group
Penguin Group (USA) Inc., 375 Hudson Street,
New York, New York 10014, U.S.A.
Penguin Books Ltd, 80 Strand,
London WC2R 0RL, England
Penguin Books Australia Ltd, 250 Camberwell Road, Camberwell,
Victoria 3124, Australia
Penguin Books Canada Ltd, 10 Alcorn Avenue,
Toronto, Ontario, Canada M4V 3B2
Penguin Book India (P) Ltd, 11 Community Centre, Panchsheel Park,
New Delhi – 110 017, India
Penguin Books (N.Z.) Ltd, Cnr Rosedale and Airborne Roads, Albany,
Auckland, New Zealand
Penguin Books (South Africa) (Pty) Ltd, 24 Sturdee Avenue,
Rosebank, Johannesburg 2196, South Africa

Penguin Books Ltd, Registered Offices:
80 Strand, London WC2R 0RL, England

First published in Penguin Books 2003

9 10 8

Grateful acknowledgment is made for permission to reprint an excerpt from *Basic, Functional and Nothing* by Eve Merriam. Used by permission of Marian Reiner.

LIBRARY OF CONGRESS CATALOGING-IN-PUBLICATION DATA

MacDonell Smith, Nancy.
The classic ten : the true story of the little black dress and nine other fashion favorites / by Nancy MacDonell Smith
p. cm.
Includes bibliographical references.
ISBN 0-14-200356-5
1. Fashion—Social aspects. 2. Costume—Symbolic aspects. 3. Fashion—History. I. Title.
GT525.M323 2003
391—dc21 2003042929

Printed in the United States of America
Set in Perpetua with Bernhard Modern • Designed by Sabrina Bowers

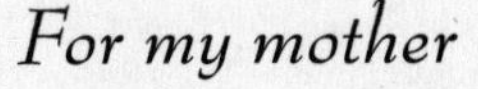

For my mother

MY HEARTFELT THANKS GO TO STÉPHANIE ABOU, MY agent, and Ann Mah, my editor, who believed in *The Classic Ten* from the moment I told them about it. Their unstinting support made this book possible. I would also like to thank two great teachers: Susie Linfield, for her insistence on "ruthless specificity," and Anne Matthews, for her endorsement of what was then the tiniest glimmer of an idea. Every writer needs good friends, and I'm blessed with many; I would particularly like to thank Annie Sommers, one of the first readers and fans of *The Classic Ten*. And finally, I would like to thank my family for their love and encouragement. This couldn't have happened without you.

Contents

Introduction

THE IDEA FOR THE CLASSIC TEN WAS BORN DURING A discussion with a professor who remarked apropos of nothing at all, "Have you ever thought of writing about fashion? You'd be good at it." I hadn't thought of it, but the suggestion not only charmed me, it made perfect sense. I spend an inordinate amount of thought and money on clothing, and this is a perfect way to justify my zeal; it's a glorious world when a new pair of shoes can be classified as research. Though I have occasional twinges of guilt about the supposed superficiality of my subject, I can't deny that my interest in it is deep and abiding. I blame this on early exposure to beautiful clothes. When I was very small, my father would return from trips to Europe with bags of clothes and shoes for my mother—lovely soft Italian knits and gleaming leather T-straps in delicious colors. I was hooked.

But far more than necklines or heel shapes, the meaning of what we wear intrigues me, particularly that of those clothes that have transcended fashion to claim icon status. The little black dress, the white shirt, the cashmere sweater, jeans, high heels, pearls, lipstick, sneakers, the suit, and the trench coat are not just garments, they're symbols that resonate across social and cultural boundaries. Their origins may be centuries old, but their meanings still ring true, because the ideas they represent—sexual allure, wealth, power, rebellion—are universal and persistent. Pearls symbolize purity, virtue, and artless perfection, while jeans are emblematic of self-expression, rock 'n' roll, and democracy. We all recognize this, just as we recognize that green means go and an olive branch signifies peace.

One reason that we're fluent in the meaning of these iconic pieces is that so many famous fashion images are built on them. Think of Audrey Hepburn staring into Tiffany's window, the personification of chic in a little black dress by Givenchy, or Marlene Dietrich smoldering in a 1930s publicity shot, wearing a man-tailored suit and a perfectly angled beret. Picture Jackie Kennedy, young and patrician-looking, in a white shirt and capris, romping on a sunlit lawn with her children, or a blue jean-clad Brooke Shields asserting that nothing came between her and her Calvins. All of these images have one thing in common: They include an iconic item of clothing. Moreover, it's the iconic items—the little black dress, the suit, the white shirt, and the jeans—that lend these images a sizable portion of their power. We immediately recognize the clothes in these photos, and we can read the myriad messages they transmit in the blink of an eye. Hepburn would not have looked nearly as memorable if she were eyeing diamonds in a duffle coat; nor would Dietrich's sexuality be as sizzling if she wore straightforward evening gowns. The little black dress, with its roots in mourning and its faint whiff of malevolence, instantly conveys an experienced worldliness; the pearls add class. The suit, so obviously borrowed from menswear, throws

Dietrich's femininity into the fore so that it's impossible to disregard.

Every item of clothing has a narrative. Some of their narratives carry greater weight, have a deeper meaning, and a more lasting influence than others. This is the story of those items.

The Classic Ten

The Little Black Dress

Women who wear black lead colorful lives.

—Neiman Marcus ad

IN ONE OF THE DELICATELY CALIBRATED SCENES IN Edith Wharton's *The Age of Innocence,* a society matron offers this biting analysis of Ellen Olenska, who has shocked 1870s New York society by her decision to divorce her husband: "What can you expect of a girl who was allowed to wear black satin at her coming-out ball?"

What, indeed? As Mrs. Archer's remark suggests, the woman in black is always suspect. Black implies you have something to hide, such as a colorful past. It's a provocative color, one few people are indifferent to. Age-old associations link it with death, evil, and destruction. Wearing black implies transgression. Anna Karenina wore black to the ball at which Vronsky became smitten with her; her niece, Kitty, herself in love with Vronsky, wore pale pink—and failed utterly to get his attention. When a woman puts on a black dress, the world assumes she's sophisticated, sexual, and knowing. By eschewing the bright plumage of the hunted for the discreet attire of the hunter the woman in black is taking on the role of the aggressor. In pastels, she's a target, passive. In black, she's charting her own course.

Seventy-five years after Wharton's fictional black gown horrified New Yorkers, Cornell Woolrich, the great pulp novelist of the 1940s, used black to turn a traditional symbol of womanhood, the bride in her white gown, into an apocalyptic vision. In *The Bride Wore Black,* Woolrich's bride, widowed on her wedding day by a car full of drunks as she and husband descended the steps of the church, is an avenging fury. She tracks down every man responsible for her husband's death, bewitches him, then kills him. In the film version Jeanne Moreau plays the bride, stalking the streets in a little black dress by Chanel, the designer who did more than any other to put women in this emphatic color.

In Ellen Olenska's time, no man wanted to marry a woman bold enough to choose black as her signature color (Ellen meets her husband not at her debut but in far less puritanical Europe, and Wharton insinuates that he is so singularly debauched that he might very well have been drawn to a girl in black) and the point of the coming-out ball was to launch debutantes into the marriage market. Yet Ellen fascinates every other character in the novel. No one remembers the white dresses of the other girls, while Ellen's raven toilette remains etched in memory. That's not surprising—black is most effective when it is surrounded by less passionate shades. Ellen's black dress symbolizes her individuality, her determination to live her life on her own terms.

It's an appealing concept, and one that has drawn generations of women to the little black dress. Indeed, the term has entered our cultural lexicon. Say it and everyone knows what you're referring to: a dress that's simple enough to appear effortless, yet elegant enough to mark the wearer as a woman of taste.

This delicious ambiguity is what makes the LBD so attractive. By turns seductive or demure, bold or self-effacing, chic or gamine, it's one of the big guns in any sartorial armory. Women as diverse as Lady Diana Spencer and Elizabeth Hurley have used LBDs to transform their public images, Diana with the low-cut ball gown she wore for her first public appearance with Prince Charles, an eye-popper that prompted headlines such as SEE NIPPLES AND DI; and Hurley with the infamous Versace safety-pin dress that catapulted her in the eyes of the world from nice English girl to smoldering sexpot.

Of course not all black is quite so sexually charged. Black also suggests a uniform chicness that transcends mere fashion. The LBD is built on refusal. It doesn't give the wearer many props, but rather lets her own self shine. It's a lot to ask from a garment, as Coco Chanel acknowledged. "Scheherezade is easy," she said. "A little black dress is hard."

Mixed with white, as in the LBD by Yves Saint Laurent that Catherine Deneuve wears in the final scene of *Belle de jour,* black's slinkiness is tempered, its purity emphasized.

Deneuve's character, a bored housewife who moonlights as a prostitute, is told that she looks like a "precocious schoolgirl" in the dress.

Black's transformative powers are astounding. Fashion magazines once trumpeted it as an excellent choice for the plump, since it is reputed to have a slimming effect. But what about black's more theatrical qualities? It can render the old sinister, the young heartbreakingly innocent, and the quiet forbidding. It's strong stuff, so potent that it can't always be faced on an empty stomach—as late as 1964, Geneviève Antoine-Dariaux warned, in her fashion etiquette book, *Elegance,* "The truly chic woman never wears black before noon."

Black is usually discouraged on girls, on the grounds that it's too worldly. Consequently, a first black dress is a milestone. My first important black dress was the one I wore to my high school graduation dance. I made it out of a piece of antique embroidered black net that I found at a vintage clothing store, and I modeled it after the dresses of the early 1920s, down to the tasseled sash that sat low around my hips. I even unearthed beaded slippers to complete my toilette. I thought I looked divine—sophisticated, mysterious, and utterly unlike anyone else I was likely to encounter that evening. My mother was not so pleased; she thought I looked like a Greek widow. But to her credit and to my gratitude, she didn't try to dissuade me from the vampy black.

Mothers and black dresses are often at odds. In Herman Wouk's 1955 novel *Marjorie Morningstar,* the heroine, like Ellen Olenska, instinctively grasps the power of black. She persuades her mother to let her wear a slinky black to a dance, when all the other girls are insipid in pastels. Thus attired, she catches the eye of a millionaire, leading her to deduce that her mother doesn't know very much about clothes.

Black is a color laden with symbolism—terms such as black heart, black magic, and blackmail indicate its dark connotations. Black is the color of sin and the supernatural. But it's also the color of asceticism, worn by the pious and the learned: Priests, nuns, scholars, hermits, and lawyers have all traditionally been shadowed in its sooty depths. Black is ideal for creating a dramatic air—Hamlet is usually depicted in black, as are the femmes fatales of both Gothic romances and film noir. Where would Rita Hayworth's Gilda have been without her black dress, or, for that matter, Mrs. Danvers, the creepy housekeeper in *Rebecca*? Both knew how to work a black dress to their advantage.

In her book *Seeing Through Clothes* the fashion historian Anne Hollander explains it might well have been this sense of drama that first launched black as a shade worn by the fashionable rather than the religious or grief-stricken. Fashionable black, she writes, did not appear until the fourteenth century, after European clothing had evolved beyond simple robes for both sexes—the implication being that only a highly sophisticated society has a need for fashionable black. In sartorial terms at least, "the Dark Ages" was a misnomer.

As the making of clothes evolved from a craft to an art, Hollander explains, "the symbolism of black could be used with creative perversity for emotional effect." In other words, anyone who dressed in clothing that was both black and fashionable was very consciously exploiting the color's contradictory traits. One of the first to mine this potential was Philip the Good, Duke of Burgundy, in the middle of the fifteenth century. Philip used sumptuous but all-black costumes to set himself apart from his colorfully dressed courtiers, an affectation that probably made him appear both saintly and satanic. In a painting of him and his courtiers, Philip looks like a foppish existentialist at a garden party. By playing a stylish version of good cop/bad cop, he no doubt kept his entourage on their toes.

Hollander also suggests that it is no accident that the rise of portrait painting in Europe coincided with the emergence of black as a fashionable shade. In its starkness, black isolates the wearer's uniqueness. Used in a portrait, it emphasizes the individual rather than rank or family connection, thereby underscoring the humanistic views of the Renaissance.

The vogue for black spread from France to Spain, where it became a favorite of the pious aristocracy. Black was also a favorite of the upwardly mobile Dutch bourgeoisie, who considered it an ideal conduit for the discreet display of wealth, as black dyes were far more expensive than any other kind.

It's interesting to note that the association of black with a solid, well-established bank account, has endured into modern times: In *Figleaf,* a humorous look at the fashion industry published in 1960, Eve Merriam included the following terms in her glossary:

BASIC: a simple black dress that costs more than $50
FUNCTIONAL: a simple black dress that costs more than $100
NOTHING: a black dress that costs more than $200
UNDERSTATED: a black dress that costs more than $300

Merriam instructs women in search of a truly chic dress to ask saleswomen to bring out something quiet and simple.

Just keep insisting, "quieter, simpler," Merriam says, and you'll eventually be presented with the priciest, most divine gown in the joint. Multiply the prices by ten and Merriam's rule still holds true.

By the sixteenth century, wearing black was no longer a way of standing out, but a way of blending in. Then, in the seventeenth century, the aristocracy, followed by the middle classes, turned to paler shades, and black became associated with dowdiness and respectability. By the nineteenth century, black had reverted to its former status as a color worn almost exclusively for mourning. But as it faded out of mainstream fashion, black's renegade past reemerged. It was adopted by the Romantics, who reveled in its dramatic mien. Black attire reinforced the image the Romantics had of themselves as lone, sensitive souls: In portraits of the era, wan-looking, black-clad young men lean pensively on one arm, looking as though they might expire from the weight of their angst. The dandies of the Romantic era were the first to wear black evening clothes, a habit that eventually became de rigueur for men of all dispositions. The demonic origins of this convention can still be seen in two figures who are, even now, represented in evening clothes: magicians and vampires.

While radical young men chose black as their emblem, for most of the nineteenth century women wore it only for mourning. The clothes of fashionable women, in contrast to soberly colored male attire, were very bright, particularly after the invention of aniline dyes in the 1850s. This emphasized the decorative role that middle- and upper-class women were relegated to in Victorian times. They stayed indoors, where their gaudy hues wouldn't get soiled. Men, dressed in somber shades that protected them from the soot and dirt of the Industrial Revolution, ventured out into the world.

One notable exception in the splashy feminine wardrobe of the time was the riding habit, which was very often black. This was a garment redolent with suggestive connotations. While not revealing, it was skintight. Based on the frock coat, and accessorized with a top hat, a white stock, and a whip, it was also severe and faintly androgynous. And, of course, it was worn while riding a horse, a veritable sexual Rorschach of an animal. Elinor Glyn, who later achieved fame as the author of racy romance novels—she wrote the Clara Bow vehicle *It*—fondly reminisced that many of her early conquests were made while she paraded in London's Hyde Park laced into a tiny-waisted habit, so small, she insisted, that even her young granddaughters couldn't fit into it.

Mourning, too, had its sexy side. Black is becoming to many complexions, and ideal for setting off the lines of the body. The mourning period lasted two and a half years with the first year and a day spent *entirely* in black. The most observant widows wore a fabric called bombazine at this stage, a textile that was renowned for absorbing rather than reflecting light, so that a woman in deep mourning looked especially severe. From this austere costume the widow moved on to black with black ornaments, and finally, subdued shades of lavender and gray, toned down with yet more black accessories. Compared to the over-the-top fashions of much of the nineteenth century, mourning clothes might very well have appeared quite smart. And unlike that other group of unavailable women, unmarried girls, widows weren't virgins. They were forbidden fruit, but ripe. A few daring women seized on the possibilities of this seductive style, and began wearing black when they wanted to appear especially memorable, whether they were in mourning or not.

An example of this enterprising audacity can be seen in John Singer Sargent's 1884 portrait of the notorious socialite Virginie Gautreau. In the painting, known as *Madame X,* Gautreau wears a smooth-as-a-glove black evening gown with a plunging décolletage and diamanté shoulder straps. With her pale skin almost lavender against the macabre bloom of the dress, she looks like a sinister orchid—self-assured and confident of her appeal. She glows with the inner satisfaction of the self-consciously well-dressed. It's a highly chic image, one that doesn't prompt any of the I-can't-believe-they-wore-that murmurs that so many historic paintings do. The unadorned black dress sets off Gautreau's haughty looks rather than obscuring them behind a flurry of ruffles and clashing colors.

Madame X caused a scandal when it was first exhibited and almost jettisoned Sargent's career. Gautreau's mother publicly despaired of her daughter's morals. Prior to the work's unveiling, Gautreau's various indiscretions had been tolerated, if frowned upon, but Sargent offended contemporary sensibilities by fetishizing her man-eating appeal. His reputation eventually recovered, but Gautreau's was irrevocably damaged. Perhaps in an attempt to undo the damage, when Sargent painted her for a second time, in 1891, Gautreau wore white, black's symbolic opposite.

Black continued to be associated with bereavement into the twentieth century. Department stores even had mourning departments, where all the necessary accoutrements could be ordered. With life expectancy still relatively low, a woman could expect to spend several years of her life in black, mourning various relatives. But it wasn't until the Black Ascot of 1910 that mourning openly attained the heights of fashion. The annual race was (and in some circles, still is) the high point of the London season, and a prime spot to parade the latest styles. It was not a place any woman would have dreamed of wearing black. However, when the high-living playboy King Edward VII died just a few weeks before the event, attendees couldn't respectfully leave it off. Newspapers of the time were filled with accounts of the marvelous black gowns that were seen. For at least one spectator, the effect was never to be forgotten: In the crowd was the young Cecil Beaton, who later created Audrey Hepburn's memorable black-and-white costume for the Ascot scene in *My Fair Lady.*

Though the terrible losses of World War I sent many women into widow's weeds, the formal, two-and-half-year observation of mourning was largely abandoned after the end of the fighting. Faced with so much death, many felt that it was best to move on.

Despite the aversion to formal mourning, World War I had accustomed the eye to two factors necessary to the widespread acceptance of the LBD, a term that was just coming into use: It was now socially acceptable to wear black on almost any occasion, and clothes had become much simpler. This was due partly to the large number of women who went to work during the war. Hampered by trailing draperies, they began to wear shorter skirts and less fussy blouses. Clothes were much smaller, too. A typical 1920s dress took two yards of fabric, compared to the ten or more necessary for prewar styles.

It's tempting to ascribe the first LBD to Chanel, because it represents everything she stood for: modernity, streamlined practically, and a quiet, self-assured sexiness that no amount of trimmings can confer. The LBD faced forward, to the future. It was worn by slim young things with shingled hair and bare legs, flappers who drank bootleg gin and rejected the suffocating fashions of their mothers. Legend has it that the couturier Paul Poiret, a man who could not adapt to the new mood of the Jazz Age, asked the black-gowned Chanel, "For whom are you in mourning, Mademoiselle?" "For you, Monsieur," was her cool reply.

Chanel had a predilection for black that was evident even in the nicknames given to her by friends, who called her both "a little black bull" and "a little black swan." Yet it's doubtful that Mademoiselle was the inventor of the LBD. When her famous design, dubbed fashion's Model T by *Vogue,* debuted in 1926, black had been seeping into fashion for several years. Chanel was famous for her self-mythologizing, however, and the story has stuck. But surely, if anyone can claim to be the LBD's spiritual godmother, it is Chanel.

Who really did invent the LBD? No one woman or man did. The LBD was a product of necessity. As women's lives became busier and their status depended less on displaying the wealth of the men they were married to, they needed clothes that were stylish but easy, chic but versatile, beautiful yet practical. The LBD fit the bill.

After the crash of 1929, the LBD's look of "poor chic" seemed particularly apt. Showy, rich-looking clothes were considered in poor taste, even among those who weathered the Depression unscathed. The clothes of the '30s were tough and no-nonsense, and black fit right in with the prevailing mood. Even Elsa Schiaparelli, whose surreal fantasies were the epitome of '30s high chic, frequently chose black as the background for her whimsical experiments.

The 1940s and 1950s were the golden age of the LBD, a time when no well-dressed woman was without one or two. In 1944, *Vogue* purred, "Ten out of ten women have one—but ten out of ten want another because the little black dress leads the best-rounded life." Fashion magazines of the post-war years are filled with images of soigné models dressed in LBDs, lipsticked, veiled, and wreathed in the smoke emanating from their still-glamorous cigarettes. Christian Dior, one of the period's most influential designers, and the creator of the New Look, captured the way women then thought about black when he said, "You can wear black at any time. You can wear it at any age. You may wear it on almost any occasion. A little black frock is essential to a woman's wardrobe."

This was also the era of intellectual and artistic black. The French entertainers Edith Piaf and Juliette Greco wore LBDs. In coffeehouses and on campuses, beatniks compounded the Left Bank look with black tights and thick black eyeliner. Like the Romantics before them, those on the fringes of society in the 1950s used black to mirror their inner states. In the popular imagination, Audrey Hepburn's pre-Paris makeover, black-jersey-wearing character in 1957's *Funny Face* was the embodiment of this style. As a mousy bookstore clerk and follower of the philosophy of "empathicalism," Hepburn was Hollywood's idea of a black-clad intellectual.

But it was Hepburn's wardrobe in another film that represented the LBD's crowning moment for millions of women. In 1961's *Breakfast at Tiffany's* Hepburn wore the same slim black Givenchy sheath in almost every scene—and always looked exactly right. The visions of Hepburn in that sublime frock and Jacqueline Kennedy in the little black dress she wore to her husband's funeral are two of the enduring images of the 1960s. In fact, Hepburn's legacy is such that thirty-three years later, when Barneys New York had the Givenchy dress copied, it sold out.

For the most part, the '60s were not a high point for the LBD. Designers turned them out, of course—both Mary Quant and André Courrèges were fans of the LBD—and older women continued to rely on them. But fashion was in too playful a mood for the serious-mindedness of black. Black was associated with maturity, and fashion was preoccupied with youth. Whether space age–influenced or flower power–enhanced, the clothes of the '60s were about the triumph of youthful sensibilities and the abandonment of convention. The old rules didn't apply anymore, in fashion or in life. With the invention of the Pill and the launch of the sexual revolution, women in black weren't the only ones promising a little naughtiness.

The nadir of the LBD came in 1968, when Cristóbal Balenciaga shut his doors, declaring he was disgusted with fashion. Like his contemporary Dior, Balenciaga was a master of the LBD. He used black over and over again—no other color set off his unparalled tailoring skills with such precision. And included in every single one of his collection was an LBD made entirely with his own hands. When she heard the news of his retirement, Mona, Countess Bismark, a legendary beauty and devotee of the LBD—Dalí painted her in one—shut herself up in her New York apartment for three days to mourn.

In the late '70s, punk rock brought black back with a roar. A dark reaction to aging rockers and leftover hippies, punk was iconoclastic in nature. The movement's fashion ground zero was Sex, Vivienne Westwood's shop on London's Kings Road. There, Westwood sold rubber fetish wear, including skintight black latex dresses: the LBD reimagined for a hostile generation.

Just as the hippie romanticism of the 1960s had moved from the street to the runway, punk's aggressive stance became a major influence on high fashion. Designers such as Claude Montana and Azzedine Alaïa, an impish favorite of the era's statuesque models, created LBDs of leather and shiny, clingy fabrics that hugged the body like an insistent caress. In the sexually charged photographs of Helmut Newton and Chris von Wangenheim, the LBD looked not so much classic as dangerous: *Madame X* taken to the extreme.

The flip side of black, its nonsexual, shroudlike aspect, came to the fore in the early '80s, with the rise of avant-garde Japanese designers such as Yohji Yamamoto and Rei Kawakubo. These designers favored clothes that hung loosely and asymmetrically on the body, and were often punctured with seemingly random cutouts. Their designs were almost always rendered in the somberest black. As Kawakubo said, "I work in three shades of black." At first, this approach was shocking—the clothes were dismissed as depressing and morbid and compared to the shapeless garments worn by bag ladies. But after their initial dismay, critics came to appreciate the ingenuity and invention of these designers. At stores like Charivari, the chicest shop in New York in the 1980s, they were top sellers. The Japanese designs cut fashion, and the LBD, loose from the retro-looking '70s and offered a modern alternative. Moreover, they ushered in a love of black that has yet to abate.

"Is there something wrong with me?" began an article in the February 2001 issue of *Lucky*. "I ask because everywhere I look I see color, color, color, and yet I seem incapable of ever purchasing any garment that isn't black." The fashionable obsession with black is now so entrenched that it's become fodder for parody. In the 2000 film *Intern*, a spoof of the fashion industry, the tantrum-throwing art director for *Skirt* magazine instructs an underling—who has already been advised to wear more black—to stay after work to redecorate everyone's desk with Philippe Starck's new office accessories line. Naturally, the entire line is black.

Why does the fashion pack love black? For the same reasons that black is such a mainstay: It's flattering, seductive, elegant, practical, engagingly louche, and reliably chic. For those who work in fashion's front lines, black takes the worry out of getting dressed in the morning because it is always correct. Other colors are promoted as alternatives to black, of course. We hear that "brown is the new black" or that gray is. But inevitably, black returns. It's better than new because it's ageless.

Carinne Roitfeld, the renowned former stylist for Gucci and now the editor of French *Vogue,* is a famous black wearer. Her signature look is a knee-length black skirt or skinny black trousers worn with a black sweater and black stilettos.

Posed with her staff in American *Vogue*'s August 2001 issue, it's clear that her influence on them is strong—all are similarly attired. They look like a force to be reckoned with: confident and formidably stylish. It's a sexy look, but Roitfeld's reason for wearing it is a mixture of the practical and the poetic. Ultimately, her reasoning lies at the core of the urban identification with black, a look that's so stark to unaccustomed eyes that first-time visitors to New York always remark on how much black New Yorkers wear.

Like the Victorian gentleman in his black frock coat, Roitfeld recognizes black as the most serviceable shade for a city dweller. But it also satisfies her aesthetic yearning to be compatible with her surroundings. She told *Vogue,* "Brown is sad. Navy blue is conservative. And black is chic. I think when you live in a town like Paris, New York or London, it's gray all year and I don't think turquoise, pink or yellow are so beautiful to mix with that weather. In the city I wear black, gray or white."

Like Roitfeld, I think black is the best color to wear in the city. But my true appreciation for black is more philosophical than practical. In black, I feel like I am wearing my clothes, rather than wondering if they are wearing me. In black, I feel comfortable, self-assured, unassailable. Against that somber screen, I feel like my self shines brightly.

The Suit

The suit seemed daring, conjuring up the same possibilities that might come from a low-cut black halter dress . . . Inspired by my attire, I asked a man to dance. "Are you going to lead?" he replied. "After all, you're wearing the pants." . . . I smiled what I imagined to be an inscrutable smile and took his hand. "We'll see," I said. "The clothes call the shots."

—Lynn Hirschberg

BACK WHEN SHE WAS MARRIED TO MICK AND A MEMBER of the international jet set, Bianca Jagger wore a lot of suits. Pantsuits, to be precise, in luscious fabrics like aubergine velvet and soft white wool. She once dined at Maxim's, the venerable Paris restaurant, in just such a pantsuit, accessorized with black mustaches painted on her cheeks, a jaunty bowler tilted over her sulky features, and a walking stick in her hand. Granted, this was in the early '70s, a time when fashion had successfully detached itself from the ordinary. Getting dressed in that era must have been like playing let's pretend every morning, with the prize going to the most willfully eccentric getup. Bianca excelled at this game. Yet what strikes me most about her is this: She never appeared ridiculous. Instead, she looked cool and perfectly turned-out and even a little aloof, as though she existed in a parallel but wildly more interesting universe. How did she pull this off? Perfect tailoring.

No matter how loopy Bianca's references got, she was grounded by her exquisite bespoke suits. They saved her from looking comic because, like all well-made suits, they exuded a sense of calm and propriety. A good suit is a triumph of structure and planning and a paean to the judicious use of artifice. It can make you look taller, thinner, more powerful, and more assured than you really are. A bad one can make you look shifty and untrustworthy, because it subverts all the themes that a good suit excels at creating.

My appreciation for suits is really a form of respect for order, workmanship, and purpose. If a suit isn't well cut and expertly constructed, no amount of surface flash can save it. A suit celebrates its maker's skill in a way that no other item of clothing can, as the fashion journalist Cathy Horyn discovered when *The New York Times* sent her to Paris to write about the experience of ordering a haute couture suit from the House of Chanel. Face to face with the highly skilled artisans who execute Karl Lagerfeld's vision, Horyn wrote, "A woman who thinks of herself as smart, who reads the magazines and wears the latest fashion, can go into a couture fitting room—where four or five people, including men, are standing around staring at her in her pathetic silk underwear (so pretty that morning)—and suddenly realize that *she knows nothing about herself.*" It's true that the process of being fitted for clothing can be discomforting, to say the least. The experienced seamstresses and tailors who staff the couture houses look on each client's body with the dispassionate eye of appraisers intent on discovering hidden flaws. The art of tailoring is nothing if not illusory, and a skilled practitioner looks on the human form as a series of problems to be solved. Horyn's finished suit fit her with both mathematical accuracy—seams had to be opened up and taken in when she wore a different bra to her first fabric fitting than she did to the initial muslin fitting—and the seductive caress of the flattering garment. When the suit arrived in New York, she "marveled that something that had taken so many hours to make and was obviously exceptional, could feel like nothing when it's on."

I doubt if I will ever have the means to join the ranks of the few thousand women in the world who buy couture suits, which today start out at roughly $15,000 (due to improved salaries and benefits for workers, a couture suit today costs ten times as much as one did in the 1960s). But I can imagine ordering a black mohair pantsuit from Jack Taylor, the Hollywood legend who has dressed such natty gents as Frank Sinatra, or buying one of Yohji Yamamoto's dramatic fitted skirt suits. In stores, I reflexively examine linings and lapels, looking for traces of the tailor's art. I like both pant- and skirt suits but I think of skirt suits as dress-up wear, whereas a pantsuit is a workhorse. Pantsuits are sleeker than their skirted sisters, like sports cars built for speed rather than luxury sedans designed to impress. For a suit to succeed it must have an element of anonymity—it shouldn't call attention to itself because its purpose is to make the body that wears it appear elegant, and elegance is never showy. Unfortunately, the anonymous skirt suit lacks any sort of spark. It makes you think of white sneakers and cold coffee and all the other aesthetically depressing aspects of the daily grind. The best skirt suits have a theatrical chic that takes them outside the realm of the everyday.

My current favorite suit is a pantsuit of very dark, somewhat stiff denim. Its perimeters are sketched with delicate white hand stitching, a sort of deluxe spin on the sturdy orange topstitching of traditional jeans. The jacket is unlined, and its curving seams are finished with white binding. Every time I put this jacket on or take it off, this small but emphatic detail delights me—the ability to elicit that kind of pure joy, however fleeting, is what defines a really wonderful article of clothing. That it is a functional part of the suit and not some added-on garnish makes its beauty all the more striking. This distinction lies at the crux of my admiration for suits.

In the language of fashion, the suit is a synonym for power. The suit is the uniform of authority, so much so that those who wield it are colloquially referred to as "suits." Like many women's garments, the suit is derived from menswear, hence its high status associations. (Men's clothes always have higher status than do women's. You have only to imagine a woman in a man's suit and then a man in an evening dress to appreciate this unfortunate truth.) In its more benign, skirted form, the suit conveys a fairly neutral type of authority; it stresses the wearer's status while subtly recalling her femininity. But a man-tailored suit on a woman is doubly provocative: It suggests both the straightforward clout of the traditional suit and the erotic implications of a woman in masculine attire. Women who have made the pantsuit their emblem—Marlene Dietrich, Katharine Hepburn, Françoise Hardy, Bianca Jagger—are seriously sexy but in an understated way. Their sexuality is an undercurrent rather than a tsunami, and they know how to swagger, just a little. A woman in a man's suit, as long as she is not trying to disguise the fact that she is a woman, is always provocative. By adopting the dress of the opposite sex, she is underscoring her own sexuality. Like black velvet against white satin, each element is thrown into high relief.

Amandine-Aurore-Lucie Dudevant, the nineteenth-century French writer who is better known by her pen name, George Sand, knew this, as did Marlene Dietrich. Both wore men's suits to devastating effect. More recently, on her *Blonde Ambition* tour, Madonna wore a rather obvious version of Dietrich's garb, a pinstriped suit with a pointy-breasted, peach-colored satin corset. The effect of the masculine banker's pinstripes against the feminine softness of the satin was perhaps flagrant compared to the relative subtlety of Sand and Dietrich, but Madonna was playing to a postmodern audience, one for whom a woman in a man-tailored suit was nothing to get excited about. She and her designer, Jean Paul Gaultier, had to push the visual metaphor to make their point. But in 1932, when Dietrich appeared in *Morocco* in her own tuxedo, the sight of her penciled brows and cupid's bow mouth above the black broadcloth was enough to titillate audiences. When she leaned in and kissed another woman, audiences in darkened movie palaces must have experienced a vicarious thrill.

Except for "breeches" roles in the theater, and a brief flirtation with Poiret's baggy harem pants in 1912, respectable women in the West had never publicly worn trousers. Amelia Bloomer's eponymous design was more sniggered at than worn. The pajama pants that came into vogue in the 1920s were intended for home wear only. Outside the house women wore skirts, as they had for thousands of years. The taboo against women in trousers was so strong that women didn't even wear two-legged underwear until the 1850s. That decade's hoopskirts, which had a tendency to capsize, made pantalets necessary if women didn't want to risk flashing passersby every time they ventured outdoors. Dietrich's deliberate flouting of convention helped to change this outdated view in the 1930s, but even more than three decades later, the more hidebound continued to discourage women from wearing pants in public. In 1964, Geneviève Antoine-Dariaux, the pedantic author of *Elegance,* scolded, "It is absolutely unaesthetic and vulgar to wear slacks on a city street, even in a raging snowstorm."

As late as the 1930s, a woman in pants could be arrested for transvestitism. Even in the 1950s, when tight-fitting toreador pants were popular for casual wear, they were not considered acceptable for work or formal occasions.

In her excellent book about the development of modern dress, *Sex and Suits,* Anne Hollander describes the relationship between male and female clothing styles as essentially idealistic: "Male and female clothing illustrates what people wish the relations between the sexes were like." In times when gender roles are impermeable, men and women dress very differently. The frock-coated mid-Victorian gentleman would never be mistaken for his wasp-waisted wife in her bell-shaped skirt. But one hundred years later, when the women's liberation movement was reaching critical mass, the unisex look was all the rage, and designers such as Pierre Cardin and André Courrèges created matching his-and-her pantsuits. Rudi Gernreich, always an envelope pusher, took this one step further by having his identically dressed male and female models shave their heads.

The man's suit, from which the woman's skirt suit and later, pantsuit, were adapted, first appeared in the late eighteenth century. Until that time, both men and women wore the type of clothing that is now associated almost exclusively with women: showy, embellished, decorative, and often impractical. Up to this point, class division rather than gender division was the key distinguishing feature of Western fashion. Men and women of the upper classes both wore unwieldy, uncomfortable clothes, including ruffs that made it difficult for the wearer to turn his or her head, trailing sleeves, high heels, and extremely heavy fabrics. At the other end of the social spectrum, working-class men and women wore much simpler, less constrictive clothing. Sumptuary laws, which laid out in microscopic detail who might wear what, kept the lower classes from trying to ape their betters.

The first Europeans to break away from this hierarchical mode of dressing were the country gentlemen of mid-eighteenth-century England, who tended to disdain foppish clothes and manners on principle, associating them with Catholicism and Continental decadence. In addition, Britain was a comparatively democratic country and democracy wreaks havoc on dress codes. While men elsewhere wore formal collarless jackets, the English squire preferred the informal and collared frock coat. And instead of bright shades of silk and velvet, he expressed his connection with the land by wearing wool, linen, and leather in earthy tones such as buff, brown, and dark green.

To his contemporaries, the English squire looked like a slob. But once the sweeping social changes that marked the end of the eighteenth century got under way, men all over Europe began emulating English style. In the aftermath of the American and French revolutions, the plain coat, jacket, and boots of the Englishmen reflected the zeitgeist far better than the silks and laces of the ancien régime. Much the same way suburban teens now appropriate elements of urban gang-banger culture, gentlemen dressed like dandified sansculottes.

The vogue for a simplified, unpretentious mode of dress was part of a widespread interest in the culture of classical Rome and Greece. Neoclassicist art, architecture, and philosophy were all the rage. Though dressmakers and tailors both responded enthusiastically to these new ideas, they expressed their ideas in radically different ways. Dressmakers, who were all women, worked by draping cloth around a pre-made corset (corsets, like all fitted garments, were made by men). Because they relied on a repertoire of improvised techniques rather than the hard-and-fast rules of measurements and patterns that tailors employed, they had wider parameters within which to indulge their whims. Dressmakers chose to interpret the neoclassic fad quite literally, putting their clients into what they considered to be faithful copies of the dresses worn by Roman matrons: narrow, gauzy muslin frocks with high waists (a style known as Empire in reference to the Roman Empire), short sleeves, and undernourished necklines. Tightly laced corsets were abandoned in favor of relatively light stays that did little to compress the figure. The aggressively modish rejected even those, preferring to pad about in the damp and drizzle of London and Paris wearing nothing but a wisp of a dress, paper-thin sandals, and a flesh-colored body stocking. Not surprisingly, sore throats and fevers were common. Jane Austen's heroines, for example, are forever taking to their beds with vague ailments. But this, too, was fashionable—the ideal woman of the early nineteenth century was pale and delicate, susceptible to the slightest chill.

The scanty attire of this period verged on public nudity. At the December 1804 wedding of Betsy Patterson to Jerome Bonaparte, a younger brother of Napoleon, a shocked male guest observed, "All the clothes worn by the bride might have been put in my pocket . . . beneath her dress she wore but a single garment." Whether the new Mrs. Bonaparte made the extra effort of damping down her gown to simulate the effect of marble drapery is unknown, but it was a popular practice. At the time, it was widely believed that catching a cold led to tuberculosis, then a common killer. Wet muslin was so associated with chills and shivers that tuberculosis was known as the muslin disease. Men, it should be noted, were not immune from this rather extreme form of vanity: Young men about town would put on their buckskin trousers soaking wet so that the pants would dry skintight. Pants left so little to the imagination in this period that they were nicknamed inexpressibles.

Instead of dressing men in updated togas, tailors approached the vogue for neoclassic dress from within their acknowledged area of expertise: the shaping of clothing to the body, a skill that was markedly different from the free-form draping and pinning, followed by the decorative placement of laces and ribbons, that dressmakers employed. It is also significant that when tailors turned to classical art for inspiration, they were confronted with the nude rather than the clothed figure. The Greeks admired modesty above all else in a woman, so women were depicted clothed. Men, for whom virility was prized, were portrayed nude. By this quirk, the perfectly proportioned nude Greek hero became the model for the modern-day business suit.

Using their shaping and piecing skills, tailors set about recreating the idealized forms delineated in works such as the Elgin Marbles, which arrived in London to great acclaim in 1806. They took the breeches and jackets that men had been wearing and slimmed them down, creating a costume that simulated idealized nudity by skimming and elongating the lines of the body. The breeches were extended to the ankle, so that the entire leg was covered in one protracted stretch of fabric. They chose to make this costume out of wool rather than the old-fashioned silk because that's what togas had been made of. This was a fortunate parallel, because wool is wonderfully pliable—through steaming, pressing, and darting it can be coaxed into any number of subtle shapes. And, unlike the stiff, heavy silks of the eighteenth century, wool drapes, creating wrinkles and folds that accentuate the movement of the arms and legs. This gave the body a new emphasis, one that was further underscored by the unified design of the suit. For instead of breaking up the structure of the body with complicated patterns, exaggerated collars, flapping pockets, and ballooning breeches, as the old styles did, the suit created the impression of a single, elegant line. If the underlying body was neither slender nor well proportioned, no matter: A skilled tailor could—and can—help almost any man fake the leggy slimness of a Greek god.

For women, the relative simplicity of the Empire line must have been exhilarating. After centuries of spreading skirts and strictly disciplined waistlines, the new silhouette was remarkably relaxed. But there had been no real change in the basic theme of women's fashion of the sort that revolutionized menswear. Women's clothes continued to be created without regard for weather and other tiresome practicalities. In contrast, men's fashion zoomed forward in the first decade of the nineteenth century and never looked back. No more outlandish hats or high heels for them—from the opening years of the new century onward, men's clothes stressed simplicity and utilitarianism. The reimagined suit, with its lack of embellishment and basis in classical ideals, came to be seen as completely natural, the style that a patriarchal God had selected for his image-sake—the way men dressed was part of the accepted order of things. And so fashion came to be thought of as a feminine concern, unworthy of masculine attention.

Indeed, men's fashion changes very little—there's not all that much difference between a nineteenth-century suit and its twenty-first-century descendent. Women in the nineteenth century, on the other hand, donned clothing that we can scarcely imagine anymore: whalebone stays, sleeves set so low the wearer couldn't raise her arms, hoopskirts that ate up six and a half yards of fabric, and bustles that protruded like bizarre and useless appendages. Unlike men's clothing, which was democratized by the arrival of the suit—when looking good means looking like a neat and tidy Greek god, one's body rather than one's income is what matters—women's clothing in the nineteenth century still continued to reflect long-standing ideas about status and wealth.

It wasn't until the 1860s that women's fashion began to take some tentative steps toward equality. This was done by approximating what men were wearing, only with a skirt. This alone made the tailor-made, or man-tailored, suit, shocking. Though no one could mistake the tailor-made for a man's suit, the extreme gender differences then the norm in fashion made it seem suspiciously masculine. Consequently, the tailor-made didn't really catch on until the 1880s, when women's roles in society were changing. Americans, who traditionally favor simpler clothing, were big fans of the tailor-made, particularly the so-called New Woman, as increasingly independent, socially visible women were known. But the tailor-made's biggest fans were the significant number of working women who found jobs in offices.

The tailor-made was intended to free women from the tyrannies of fashion. Yet women who wore them had to walk a fine line between looking capable and looking unfeminine. A *Ladies' Home Journal* article of 1907 titled "As Business-women Should and Should Not Dress," summed up this quandary by labeling a woman who dressed too severely as ". . . a feeble imitation of a man," a "he-female." On the other hand, the article continued, looking too attractive was equally dubious: ". . . the woman of sense doesn't go to her office in a peek-a-boo waist [a blouse with sheer sleeves] and a trailing velveteen skirt."

The suit had a look of efficiency that made it easier for women to be taken seriously. But beneath their functional-looking tailoring, women were more constrictively laced than ever. The early-twentieth-century S-bend silhouette, which pushed both the buttocks and the breasts down and out, required a long-line corset that made it difficult to take a normal stride. It wasn't until after World War I that women were as free beneath their clothes as they appeared on the outside. That was when Coco Chanel achieved widespread fame with her sophisticated separates and chic little suits. In her mission to modernize women's clothing, Chanel turned to the same model that late-eighteenth-century tailors did when they modernized men's clothes: the English gentleman. Since meeting up with Boy Capel, her aristocratic English lover and financial backer, in 1908, she had borrowed extensively from his wardrobe of tailored tweeds and flannels. In these streamlined garments she was her own best model, creating a look of pared-down elegance that women all over the world copied.

Thanks to Chanel and innovators like her, the suit became a staple of women's wardrobes, particularly women who worked. Suits were a favorite costume of the women's pictures of the 1930s and 1940s, films in which actresses such as Joan Crawford and Bette Davis triumphed over some social setback or disease, all the while perfectly turned out in tailored jackets and skirts. The suit was a symbol of adulthood, a uniform that separated the women from the girls. By the mid-1950s, recalled Mary Cantwell, the author of

Manhattan, When I Was Young, and then a young magazine editor, a suit was a rite of passage, as far removed from a coed's plaid skirt as a tie was from short pants: "One Saturday afternoon we strolled through the College Shop at Lord & Taylor, checking out the Shetland sweaters and the Bermuda shorts and the camel's hair polo coats, sorrowful that they would never be ours again and even a little frightened. We had outgrown them . . ." To solve her dress dilemma, Cantwell "bought a length of green tweed, took it to a tailor on West Seventy-second Street . . . and had it made up into a stern suit which I believed announced intelligence as well as chic."

Needless to say, the suit Cantwell had made included a skirt. In terms of modernity, women's clothes had progressed, but the New Look was a stumbling block. Christian Dior's designs were gorgeous but almost as impractical as the Belle Epoque contours he loved. In response, an irate Chanel came out of retirement, railing against male designers who deformed women with their mad ideas. She then sat down and created the style that she is best remembered for, the cardigan suit. Variations of this refined, flattering ensemble became the uniform of middle-aged ladies all over the world, a life preserver that they clung to through the fashion storm of the 1960s.

Though the miniskirt is the garment most commonly associated with that decade, the pantsuit was arguably its most revolutionary fashion development. The mini was after all still a skirt, a variation of something women had been wearing for thousands of years. Pants were new territory and they made people nervous. In 1966, the year Yves Saint Laurent sent his first pantsuit down the runway, one woman, a math professor, had her mother tell her that she shouldn't wear a pantsuit to work because the students "will be able to tell that your legs go all the way up." Presumably this professor's students would be able to deduce that from her miniskirts, but her mother's concern was far from uncommon.

Schools, businesses, and many restaurants prohibited women from wearing pants, though determined women defied the ban. Judy Carne, an actress on *Laugh-In,* showed up for dinner at '21' wearing pants and a tunic. She was stopped by the maître-d', who told her that '21' didn't seat women in pants. Carne calmly stepped out of her pants and continued into the restaurant in her revealing yet noncontroversial tunic-cum-micromini. Restaurateurs got the message, and most revised their dress codes.

Saint Laurent's *le smoking,* named after the French term for tuxedo, was the most sophisticated of the new pantsuits. Alice Rawsthorn, Saint Laurent's biographer, describes how before the advent of *le smoking* pantsuits were associated mainly with mannish women such as Gertrude Stein. A few iconoclasts had worn them, but for the most part those who did were celebrities who could be forgiven such eccentricities. A civilian pantsuit wearer was more likely to get reactions akin to that of the math professor's scandalized mother. Saint Laurent softened the tuxedo's cut, making it less adamantly masculine. On the runway, he showed the *smokings* with stiletto heels, lushly painted lips, and sheer blouses, details that further underscored the *smokings'* newly revealed femininity. Such juxtapositions are commonplace today, but Saint Laurent was breaking new ground. The response, writes Rawsthorn, was thundering. "An Yves Saint Laurent *smoking* became the uniform for the new generation of women who, by appropriating a masculine style, were signaling that they did not intend to defer to men as second class citizens."

In a pantsuit, a woman could be both a siren and businesswoman—a combination that was played up in one of the most famous ad campaigns of the 1970s, for Charlie perfume. The ads focused on women in YSL-style suits, striding all over a city that was theirs for the taking.

While Saint Laurent reveled in femininity, another '70s tastemaker, John T. Molloy, sought to keep it under wraps. Molloy was the author of the 1977 book *The Woman's Dress for Success Book,* which he grandiosely called "the most important book ever written about women's clothes." Molloy warned women that the fashion industry was not on their side. The more fashionably a woman dressed, according to Molloy, the less likely she was to climb the corporate ladder. He counseled against wearing pantsuits to the office because they were too masculine and newfangled. Molloy also panned long hair, frilly blouses, and conspicuous makeup. If a woman wanted to do well in business, he wrote, she needed to wear a navy blue skirt suit and keep her hair above her shoulders. To keep coworkers from forgetting her gender, she should add a floppy bow tie.

Molloy's book unleashed a navy-skirted army—but as with any huge trend, there came a proportionately epic backlash. By 1985, *The New York Times* ran a cover story hailing the end of dress for success. The *Times* quoted Mary Fiedorek, the author of a rival dress etiquette book, *The Executive Style: Looking It, Living It.* According to Fiedorek, women had been "brainwashed . . . into thinking that executive wear is synonymous with a suit." The problem was that by that point, pretty much every woman over twenty was wearing a suit. The suit's impact had been diluted, and the search was on for a new power uniform. Designers tinkered with the suit, making it tighter and shorter, and churning it out in bright colors like red and yellow. At one point, women were sending out a weird dual message, says Alison Lurie in *The Language of Clothes.* With their quarterback-sized shoulder pads, they looked quite impressive sitting behind a desk. But the moment they stood up and revealed their thigh-baring skirts, they looked like anxious-to-please little girls. Women who didn't want to struggle with this questionable look turned to designers such as Giorgio Armani and Donna Karan, who relaxed stern tailoring with their fluid, languorous lines. Both Armani and Karan were fans of the pantsuit, an increasingly popular choice in the early '90s: According to *The New York Times,* between 1990 and 1995, sales of women's pantsuits grew 167 percent.

Today, very few women I know favor skirt suits. Only those with very stuffy jobs feel obliged to wear them. For the moment, the daytime skirt suit is a relic of an earlier age, like pantyhose and floppy bow ties. Designers such as Helmut Lang, Nicolas Ghesquière, and Hedi Slimane (who actually designs for men but is a favorite of chic women) make pantsuits that are in tune with the way women want to look now: sleek, capable, and self-assuredly sexy (and, I might add youthful: with their shrunken shoulders and skinny thighs, these suits are boyish rather than mannish). Their suits are utterly modern, a quality that lies at the core of the suit's appeal. Furthermore, at a time when the pace of fashion is so ferocious—the shelf life of each season's must-have look seems to average about five minutes—the suit offers sass, intelligence, and staying power.

On the occasion of her fiftieth birthday, Isabella Rossellini was photographed for *In Style*. The actress chose to wear a pinstriped suit for her portrait, saying: "There are a lot of beautiful things that are too hard to wear; tight skirts, high heels. I'll wear them out if I know I'll be home in two hours, but most days I'm out from eight A.M. to seven P.M. Men's suits have become my solution. They are incredibly comfortable and sexy."

Rossellini's sentiments represent a complete turnaround from the negative, faux-masculine image the man-tailored suit was saddled with by pundits such as John Molloy. This point was driven home by the recent appearance of two successful actresses—Angelina Jolie and Jennifer Aniston—in man-tailored suits. Jolie, in pristine white, and Aniston, in sophisticated black, wore their suits to awards shows, venues that normally call for the tightest, plungiest evening gowns a stylist can unearth. Both went bare beneath their jackets, and both looked fabulous: sexy, confident, and insouciant. By treating their sexual appeal casually, as though they knew its worth and didn't care if anyone else did, they made it clear that they were comfortable with themselves. The suit became a conduit for feminine sexuality rather than a shroud.

Jolie and Aniston's cool gusto reminded me of one of my favorite photographs. The photo was taken by Helmut Newton in the summer of 1975, in the rue Aubriot, in the Marais section of Paris. The subject is a slender woman in a man-tailored suit. The suit is dark, strict—severe, even. It is Saint Laurent's *le smoking,* of course. The woman's hair is parted on the side and slicked back. She does not face the camera. Rather, she's looking down, her expression pensive. She rests one hand in the pocket of her trousers and cups a cigarette in the other, holding it with the practiced ease of a world-weary boulevardier. Hers is a man's pose, dapper and devil-may-care. Unlike most fashion photo subjects, she makes no attempt to engage or even acknowledge the viewer. She is self-contained and impervious to the click of the shutter. Yet no matter how many times I revisit this image, she never fails to hold my eye. The woman in the suit radiates self-confidence. This effect is bolstered by her slightly defiant stance, but its ultimate source is her attire. The model who posed for Newton, Vibeke Bergeron, later said, "I never wanted any of the clothes I wore until I put on that Saint Laurent suit. It felt good, and I felt that I looked fantastic. I felt edgy, but I also felt beautiful." After that, she reported, she began to wear pantsuits, and does to this day.

I understand Bergeron's feelings exactly: She wears suits because she feels invincible in them. It's this quality that has earned this photograph its slot in my fashion menagerie, and the pantsuit pride of place in my closet.

Jeans

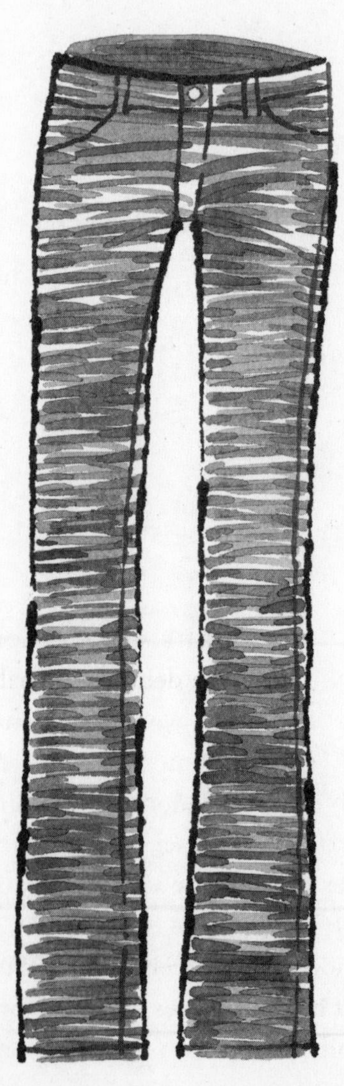

Blue denim is America's gift to the world.

—Charles James

THIS REMARK, ONE OF THE MORE PERCEPTIVE OBSERVATIONS ever made about denim, is attributed to a man who probably never in his life wore jeans. Charles James, the Harrow-educated son of an American mother and an English father, is generally regarded, along with Mainbocher, as one of the only American couturiers—which is to say that he hand-made clothes to order for a select clientele. He worked from the early 1930s through the early 1970s, though his most prolific period was the 1940s and 1950s, a time when café society was at its peak. James designed for women whose lives were a round of lunches, nightclubs, and summers on the Riviera. His specialty was the fabulously expensive evening dress, which he cut with biomorphic flair: One slinky black satin specimen from the late '30s is ornamented with spiky, pinwheel-shaped bursts of fabric on either side of the wearer's pelvis; similarly sharp points rear up and away from the breasts. The whole thing brings to mind a gorgeous, freshly satiated praying mantis.

A James original—the women who wore them called them "Charlies" and bought extra airplane seats for them—could take two years to make. James was an exacting perfectionist, willing to rip a dress apart if he found one crooked stitch. His need to control his creations was so great that it didn't end even when they left the workroom. He once refused to make a gown for a London hostess because he thought her frumpy and awkward and he didn't care to see his clothes on such a graceless woman.

Not exactly the kind of guy you could picture relaxing in well-worn 501s, a cold Budweiser in his hand. But James had the imagination and understanding to recognize the quintessentially American quality of denim. He worked with silk, the most aristocratic of fabrics, but he recognized denim as the sartorial symbol of democracy.

Jeans are the antithesis of couture, which is built on a rigid etiquette of fittings and is beyond the reach of all but a very few. The most famous photograph of James's work, shot by his childhood friend Cecil Beaton and published in *Vogue* in 1948, shows a group of women clad in his elaborately shaped and cinched ball gowns, which gleam expensively in the light. The scene could be a gathering of ladies-in-waiting painted by Franz Xavier Winterhalter (1805–73), the chronicler of court life during the era of the crinoline. The women are holding demitasse cups and are gathered in a room that can only be described as a salon. There aren't any men present, and since these look like the kind of women who marry often and well, we can presume that the husbands are still at the dinner table, drinking port and discussing world affairs. It is a scene of now-lost luxury, closer to the mannered world of Henry James than the atomic age. The women in the photo are representative of the quintessential Charles James client: moneyed, sophisticated, indulged. Their dresses, made of costly silks and velvets that are exquisitely draped and cut, are designed to display these qualities, a practice that the social theorist Thorstein Veblen termed conspicuous consumption. If these women were wearing jeans, we would have a much more difficult time identifying them as members of the moneyed class. Couture separates the haves from the have-nots; jeans break down the barrier.

As Kennedy Fraser, a fashion critic for *The New Yorker,* wrote in 1971, "the potential elegance [of jeans] does not depend on wealth." Jeans purchased for $39.99 at Gap and those bearing designer names and four-figure price tags hold forth the same promise. A pair of jeans is a talisman, imbued with the qualities that they have become equated with: individualism, coolness, rebellion. Their cachet is informed not by the wearer but by denim's own mythology.

There's something about slipping on a pair of jeans that gives one an aura of instant, effortless stylishness. This stems partly from their cut, which emphasizes the hips and thighs, and sexily packages the crotch between two J-shaped pockets; and partly from their chameleonlike ability to look good with everything from a T-shirt to a boned corset, a combination that jeans lover and rock-star progeny Stella McCartney—daughter of Beatle Paul—has helped turn into a uniform for fashionable young women around the world.

McCartney's heritage and her fondness for denim go hand-in-hand—jeans and rock 'n' roll are as natural a combination as wine and cheese, or basic black and pearls. Rock stars are perceived as rebels, as are cowboys, bikers, and hippies, some of the other groups we associate with denim. Put on a pair of jeans, the thinking goes, and a little bit of their outlaw glamour will rub off on you. Jeans are a way of symbolically thumbing your nose at bourgeois ideas about proper dress, and asserting that you're casual, carefree, youthful, a rebel at heart, and not one to be stifled by convention. Now that jeans are acceptable attire pretty much everywhere, this message has been diluted somewhat. But when politicians and celebrities want to show that they're just folks, they still wear jeans.

The archetypal blue jeans are Levi's, particularly the button-fly, shrink-to-fit 501s that the company has been producing for more than a hundred years. Levi Strauss, the Bavarian immigrant who stitched the first pair, didn't set out to create a fashion empire. He went West with the gold rush in the 1850s and opened a dry goods store. It proved faster to make pants and other work gear for the miners on the premises rather than shipping them from the East, so Strauss got into the clothing business. He had been making canvas pants for several years when he received a note from Jacob Davis, a tailor from Reno, Nevada, in 1873. Davis had the bright idea of riveting the pockets of work pants to make them stronger. He suggested that Strauss go into business with him, speculating that the two "could make a very large amount of money" by patenting the new and improved pants. Strauss took out a patent, stitched the back pocket of his blue-dyed trousers with two wavy lines he dubbed the Arcuate Design, and unwittingly stepped into history. The 501 designation dates from 1890, when the company began assigning lot numbers to its various styles.

The road from work gear to symbol of stylish nonconformity began in the West and moved east. From company headquarters in San Francisco, Levi Strauss and Co.'s sales force traveled all over the western United States, selling pants, jackets, and coveralls to the small dry goods stores that outfitted the local workforce, including cowhands from the region's many ranches. Comfortable and tough enough to withstand days in the saddle, the waist overalls—until 1960, the official name of Levi's jeans—and denim jackets quickly became the cowboy's unofficial uniform.

(It should be noted, however, that in spite of the popular association of Levi's and cowboys, real cowboys prefer Wrangler. That's because Wrangler jeans were designed with cowboys' needs in mind, such as higher pockets so they won't sit on their wallets while on horseback, smooth rivets that won't scratch saddle leather, and extra belt loops to accommodate the heft of western-style belts. As of 1997, 98 percent of Professional Rodeo Association riders wore Wranglers.)

While westerners were quick to adopt jeans as a comfortable form of casual clothing, easterners were more conventional. They pretty much ignored denim until the 1930s, when two factors brought the work wear of the West to a wider audience. One was the Hollywood western, which elevated the workaday cowboy and his signature clothing to heroic stature. As epitomized by Gary Cooper, Tom Mix, and a host of other square-jawed actors, the cowboy came to symbolize idealized manhood. Celluloid cowboys were inevitably handsome, straight-shooting, rugged individualists who were also kind to women and children (though they rarely did anything as sissy as kissing a girl). Millions of little boys, and no doubt quite a few little girls, dreamed about growing up to be cowboys. Cowboy costumes, which included fringed vests, bandannas, Stetson-style hats, and the inevitable dungarees, were popular with American children from the 1930s through the 1950s.

The other factor that contributed to denim's growing popularity was the inception of the dude ranch. Strapped for cash during the Depression, ranchers in California, Nevada, and Arizona began to rent rooms to vacationing, middle-class easterners. Once they arrived on the ranch, these aspiring cowboys wanted to look the part, so they bought the requisite gear at the local general store. They took their new purchases back East with them, where they became acceptable casual clothing.

The amateur ranchers included women, a market that up until then had been largely ignored by denim manufacturers. For the most part, if women wanted to wear jeans, they were obliged to make do with cuts intended for men. In 1935, Levi's responded to this new market by launching Lady Levi's, part of the Dude Ranch Duds line. Lady Levi's were cut with smaller waists and more generous hips to flatter feminine figures. That same year, jeans made their first appearance in a fashion magazine, when *Vogue* featured a story on dude-ranch fashions.

Jeans also began to appear on noncowboys in films, though rarely on female characters. An exception was *The Women,* released in 1939 and based on Clare Boothe Luce's play of the same name. In the film, the main characters, a group of sharp-tongued New York socialites, head to a Nevada dude ranch to take advantage of the state's liberal divorce laws.(If a woman could prove that she was a resident of Nevada—that is, had lived there for six months—she could be free of her spouse relatively quickly, rather than having to wait out the two years required in most other places. A Reno divorce was a common practice among those who could afford it, who referred to it as being "renovated.") Outfitted in well-tailored, well-accessorized denim, they lounge around complaining about men and scheming to land their next husbands.

In 1943, prompted in part by the fabric restrictions imposed by the government in response to World War II, American Claire McCardell became the first designer to include denim in her collection. Denim, along with heavy woolens and other menswear materials, had previously been considered inappropriate for women's clothing. But McCardell had been an advocate of simplicity and practicality from the beginning of her career in the early 1930s and she had a natural affinity for inexpensive and unusual materials. She firmly believed that clothes should be easy to care for as well as attractive and stuck to practical fabrics and straightforward cuts. Consequently, the fabric restrictions weren't a hardship for McCardell, as they were for many designers, but a challenge.

It was during the war years that American sportswear, which would pave the way for the casualness of jeans dressing, came into its own. Cut off from Paris, American designers were forced to fall back on their own resources. Instead of aping Parisian couture, they began to design less fussy clothes that were better suited to the active lifestyles of American women. McCardell was at the forefront of this movement (a few years later, the feminist Betty Friedan, then a writer for women's magazines, described McCardell as "the girl who defied Dior"). She created the denim Popover dress, which came with an attached potholder, for women who were facing a servant shortage due to the war and had to cook and serve dinner themselves. Comfortable and flattering, the dress was an instant best-seller. McCardell also made a denim coverall that could be worn over other clothes with the many new female factory workers in mind. The coverall was shot by *Harper's Bazaar* in 1943, on a young model named Betty Bacall, a rookie whose healthy radiance was reminiscent of McCardell's own rangy blonde looks. Indeed, many of McCardell's models shared her look; it was one ideally suited to the sporty sensibility of her designs.

In contrast to heavily made-up, floral-and-flounce-wearing starlets such as Lana Turner, Bacall was fresh and unadulterated looking; she appeared as clean-limbed and lovely in jeans as she did in an evening dress. Most important, her lack of artifice and utterly natural demeanor, always appealing to Americans, seemed especially appropriate as the country entered World War II.

One of Bacall's modeling shots was spotted by socialite Slim Keith, a devotee of scrubbed-clean chic. Slim recommended that her then-husband, Howard Hawks, cast Bacall opposite Humphrey Bogart in his upcoming film, *To Have and Have Not.* Hawks had based Bacall's character on his wife, even naming her Slim. As Bacall, rechristened Lauren, portrayed her, she was a tough-talking cutie with an independent streak. Her best-known line in the film, "You know how to whistle don't you? Just put your lips together and blow," is a classic of the era, redolent of the plucky spirit of its film heroines.

Slim—the nickname came courtesy of matinee idol William Powell; she was born Nancy Gross—was herself a jeans wearer. She was even photographed for *Harper's Bazaar* wearing her own jeans and a denim work shirt ordered from the Sears catalog, looking so captivating that women across the country were prompted to incorporate denim into their wardrobes. Later named by Truman Capote as one of his stylish Swans—the others were Babe Paley, Gloria Guinness, and C. Z. Guest—Slim was the original California girl. She radiated a relaxed, sun-kissed chic. At the farm she shared with Hawks, Slim, casually turned out in striped T's and aviator shades, played hostess and fishing buddy to luminaries such as Ernest Hemingway and Cary Grant. As she explained in her memoir, *Slim: Memories of a Rich and Imperfect Life,* "In my day, different meant not having your hair done in a pompadour and adorning it with a snood, or not trying to hide your intelligence behind a sea of frills. I somehow knew there was a glut in that market. I opted for a scrubbed-clean, polished look. I thought it was more important to have an intelligence that showed, a humor that never failed, and a healthy interest in men."

Slim Keith was the opposite of the languorous women photographed by Cecil Beaton. If Beaton's women suggested the Europhile heroines of Henry James, then Slim evoked F. Scott Fitzgerald's golf-playing Jordan Baker, whom the author described as wearing her evening clothes with the casual assurance of sports clothes. Slim was active, spirited, independent, subtly sexy, and unlikely to wear anything that was merely pretty. Her clothes had to keep up with her and her lifestyle. McCardell could have been describing Slim when she explained what inspired her designs: "For me it is American—what looks and feels like America. It's freedom, it's democracy, it's casualness, it's good health. Clothes can say all that." And no item says that with more emphasis than jeans.

But while Slim Keith made slipping into a pair of jeans and tooling around barefoot seem downright seductive, to others the trend toward casual dress was evidence of a serious decline in standards. In 1949, trying to expand nationwide and needing to appeal to an audience beyond the farm, Levi's devised an ad campaign with the tag line, "Denim: Right for School." The result was a flood of hate mail from irate parents who were horrified at the thought of jeans in the classroom. Some went so far as to try to link denim with juvenile delinquency.

Another antidenim crusader of the '50s was designer Anne Fogarty. Fogarty, who was definitely not of the McCardell school of thought, wrote a book called *Wife Dressing* in which she chastised women for wearing jeans. Though she reluctantly conceded that the hated dungarees were practical for certain heavy household chores, she cautioned her readers, "Don't look like a steamfitter or a garage mechanic when what you are, purely and simply, is a wife."

As Fogarty's advice suggests, gender roles were very rigid in the 1950s. Stepping outside them was a rebellious act. One way to do this was through clothing, and jeans, with their association with individuality, were an ideal outlet. The popularity of jeans with the young was ensured with the release of two films in the mid-'50s, *Rebel Without a Cause* and *The Wild One.* Both featured young, alienated, jeans-wearing heroes—James Dean and Marlon Brando, respectively—and provided much darker and more realistic screen portrayals of adolescence than earlier films. (Andy Hardy certainly never wore jeans.) Both men became teen idols, and their fans paid homage to them by dressing just like them, in denim. Dean in particular was ensured a place in the pantheon of cool by his early death in a car crash. He died with his jeans on.

For boys, jeans and a T-shirt became a ubiquitous uniform, while girls topped their dungarees with men's shirts, imitating Marilyn Monroe's sexy look in 1954's *River of No Return.* In Europe and Japan, where jeans had been introduced by GIs during World War II, teens were similarly besotted. In the postwar years American culture was just beginning its ascent to the position of influence it occupies today, and the young were the first to feel its pull. In the 1954 Italian film *Un Americano a Roma,* the young Roman protagonist, a wannabe American, wears jeans as evidence of his supposed Yankeeness.

By the 1960s, jeans were a badge of membership in the counterculture. But instead of the dark, uniform look of '50s denim, '60s denim was personalized with beading, embroidery, appliqué, and elaborate patchwork to make it look more individual. The idea was that jeans should be anything but new and similar. Self-expression was the war cry of the younger generation, and dress was a tool in the battle against conformity. Embellished blue jeans stood for the opposite of everything the ubiquitous gray flannel suit of the '50s embodied. Marshall McLuhan summed up the '60s attitude toward denim when he said, "Jeans represent a rip-off and rage against the establishment."

Jeans manufacturers responded to this sea change in their market by aiming their advertising at the young. Levi's, which had once advertised solely in ranch and agricultural publications, commissioned posters that borrowed from artist Peter Max's psychedelic style. In 1967, Jefferson Airplane appeared in a Levi's TV commercial, performing a version of their hit "White Rabbit."

As the '60s gave way to the '70s, jeans were a part of the international landscape. On a stroll down Fifth Avenue in the summer of 1971, Kennedy Fraser, *The New Yorker* fashion critic, noted, "Apart from the men in business suits, the largest group of people I came across was wearing blue jeans. The kids who wear them often look as tediously uniform as their fathers; tie-dyed T-shirts, headbands, and denim, are, of course, blind emblems of a way of life quite as much as seersucker jackets and button-down collars." The counterculture had been so successful at spreading its message of rebellion through dress that jeans were now as common as the gray flannel suit had once been.

Denim was no longer a symbol of the cowboy, the rebel, or the hippie, but the cloth of choice for an increasingly casual society. Because jeans were emblematic of a lifestyle that was free of middle-class trappings, by wearing them everyone was able to "drop out" a little bit, even if the most controversial thing he or she had ever done was to return a library book late. Consequently, denim was the most popular fabric of the decade.

When I started school in the mid-'70s not only did most of the students wear jeans—the few who didn't invariably had older or noticeably conservative parents—but the teachers did, too. My parents, who were young, wore jeans—I particularly liked a pair of my mother's bell-bottoms, because the braided belt loops seemed so exotic. My first pair of jeans were made by UFO and had side zippers instead of the traditional five-pocket cut. I loved them and had to be forced to wear girly things like dresses. Twenty-five years earlier, about the same time Levi's was being attacked for its inflamatory "Right for School" campaign, my mother wore dresses even when rollerskating.

In response to the increased demand for denim and all it conveyed, manufacturers had expanded their wares to include denim leisure suits, denim sheets, and even a denim-upholstered car, GM's Gremlin. In 1971, Andy Warhol put a close-up of a denim-clad crotch, complete with working zipper, on the cover of the Rolling Stones album *Sticky Fingers.* Far from decrying the spread of denim, that same year, the fashion industry presented Levi Strauss & Co. with its equivalent of the Oscar, the Coty Award. Department stores, which hadn't yet deigned to carry denim, began to stock it. What had started out as antifashion was now an important part of fashion.

In *What We Wore,* Ellen Melinkoff observed that while women in the '70s could "wear anything, anywhere—all they wanted to wear was jeans." This predilection was fed by the rise of the designer jean, which was distinguished from its plebian forebear by the designer logo emblazoned on the back pocket. Among the names that decorated buttocks in the '70s were Calvin Klein, Gloria Vanderbilt, Fiorucci, Jesus Jeans, Sergio Valente, and Studio 54. (The poster showed a naked man pulling on a pair of jeans, with a tag line that read, "Now everybody can get into Studio 54.") Designer jeans cost two or three times as much as regular jeans, and in order to preserve their deep indigo hue, they had to be dry-cleaned. They were also supposed to be worn skintight. A photo taken at the Fiorucci store on Fifty-ninth Street in the '70s of two salesmen helping a woman zip up her jeans illustrates what an ordeal this could be: One salesman is standing behind the woman, holding the two sides of the zipper together, while the other faces her as he struggles to do it up. None of this prevented fashion junkies of both sexes from rushing out to buy designer denim.

Since an extended interest in one item of clothing can spell trouble for the fashion industry, designers began to vary their cuts from season to season. Legs were tight one year, wide the next; cuffs were turned up, then folded under. There was even a brief craze for see-through jeans. To be out of step with that season's style was disastrous. Advertising focused on the sexiness of jeans, culminating in Brooke Shield's famous assertion that nothing came between her and her Calvins. Instead of peasant tops and work boots, jeans were paired with silk blouses and disco sandals. Denim had grown far away from its proletarian roots.

As the disco era faded, so did the prestige of designer denim. By the mid-'80s, designer jeans were rejected as cheesy. Acid wash, one of the innovations to denim made by the fashion industry, was dismissed as tacky before it ever got off the ground. Consumers wanted authenticity, not flash. Vintage denim was in demand, the rarer the better, with perfectly faded 501s the Holy Grail of the flea market pilgrim. In 1995, *Vogue* published a piece on the international used-denim trade, including a guide to Levi lingo, such as "big Es" to refer to a pair of pre-1971 501s, which have a capital E in the red Levi's tag. The story focused on the high price paid for pristine old school denim: "ARE YOUR JEANS WORTH $10,000?" a cover line asked.

By the mid-'80s, jeans were so comfortably ensconced in the world's closets that they were once again antifashion rather than fashion. Unlike the designers of the '70s, who created entire denim wardrobes, the designers of the '80s weren't terribly interested in denim. The social climate had shifted, and consumers were in the mood to dress up, not down. They wanted to show off their newfound wealth, a practice that earned the '80s the nickname "the greed decade."

The fashion most associated with the '80s is the pouf skirt, a sort of voluminous, cream-puff-shaped miniskirt created by Christian Lacroix. A favorite of the newly named yuppie woman, Lacroix was hailed as the savior of couture, which had floundered during the dress-down '70s. Lacroix's clothes were the ultimate in conspicuous consumption, replete with hooped skirts, extravagant ruffles, huge poufs of fuchsia and canary yellow silk, and lavish bows. They fit in with the prevailing sensibility, which held that hiding one's wealth in ordinary blue jeans was no fun. Lacroix's style was even referenced as a symbol of the decade's gimme-gimme money culture; in Tom Wolfe's novel *The Bonfire of the Vanities,* the wife of a Wall Street bond salesman who thinks of himself as a "Master of the Universe" is described as wearing a dress with "puffed sleeves the size of Chinese lanterns." Not everyone had it so good, of course; it was in the '80s that homelessness in America reached new highs. When the stock market crashed on the same day in 1987 that Lacroix opened a New York boutique, some saw it as a portent that the good times were coming to an end.

Sure enough, the economic outlook darkened, and clothes became much more sober—one of the major trends of the '90s was minimalism and a return to basic black. While the clothes of the '80s were too flashy and fantastic for denim to gain much of a foothold in fashion, the '90s were ripe for a denim revival.

The first wave of '90s fashion denim was dark and stiff, similar to the pristine denim of the '50s in all but its high price, which, for a pair of high-status jeans by a designer such as Helmut Lang, could be several hundred dollars. But the denim wave really started to gather momentum in the wake of Gucci's "Cher goes to Vegas" spring 1996 collection. The collection's showpiece was a pair of faded and embellished jeans, which ushered in a vogue for the rich hippie look (very rich—Gucci's jeans sold for thousands of dollars). The fad for embellishment faded after a season, but the demand for denim—aged, dark, or deliberately dirty-looking—remains high. Denim is once again conspicuously cool. As in the heydays of the '70s, dozens of new jeans labels have emerged, including Earl; Seven; Frankie B; Paper, Denim & Cloth; and Juicy Jeans, each claiming to have the most flattering cut. Top designers have scrambled to add denim lines to their collections, and jeans can be seen on runways from Versace to Chanel. Henry Duarte, dubbed the "Yves Saint Laurent of rock 'n' roll" by *Harper's Bazaar,* was a California designer who had been making elaborately pieced, custom-order jeans and leather pants for rock stars for ten years. When the denim craze took off, he found himself with a new clientele of starlets and fashionistas.

Duarte's one-of-a-kind creations are the zenith of the craze for unique clothing that has emerged in response to an increasingly global, homogenized society. Studded appliquéd jeans are once again making the scene, appearing at Hollywood premieres and downtown Manhattan hotspots. Denim behemoths such as Levi's, which was once considered the epitome of cool, have come to be associated with middle-aged baby boomers. Smaller labels, such as Habitual, are preferred among denim cognoscenti. Where denim's wide availability and cloth-of-the-people status were once its coolness signifiers, today's hippest denim is more exclusive, a sort of trophy for those in the know. Though denim went through a designer phase in the '70s, today's indie denim labels stay away from the kind of advertising that was common then. An air of exclusivity is preferred.

Another distinguishing feature of the new wave of denim is its very feminine sexiness. Jeans are essentially a masculine item of clothing. But women have claimed denim as their own, and are demanding it be cut to their specifications—

two popular denim lines, Earl and Frankie B., were started by women who couldn't find jeans that fit the way they wanted them to. Women want the comfort of denim and the sexiness of stilettos, and more and more are pairing the two.

Stella McCartney, who always has jeans on her runway, has said that she designs her collections around the way she likes to dress: jeans, a little-nothing top, and sexy heels are her fashion perennials. Go to any gathering in New York, London, or Los Angeles and you'll see scores of similarly attired young women. They're not exactly McCardell-ites but neither are they as trussed-up as James's girls. For the moment, at least, the two extremes have called a truce.

For myself, the perfect pair of jeans remains an elusive prize; I don't know if such a treasure exists. Every pair I own or admire has some charateristic that enthralls me. I love perfectly faded indigos, pockets that curve with the body, time-softened flanks, legs that flare just so over the instep of a pointed boot. Like a hopeless womanizer, I don't know if I could ever commit to one pair. Even when I find jeans that fit with the requisite mix of pocket and fade, the question of length remains. Should I hem them to wear with high or low heels? Perhaps, as one magazine recently suggested, I should buy two pairs and hem one for heels and the other for flats. But such profligacy seems antithetical to the spirit of denim. And that's what really draws me to jeans—their lack of artifice. I like solutions that are simple yet elegantly wrought, and that's what jeans offer. For while I admire the baroque styling of Charles James, it's Claire McCardell's fresh-faced practicality that I could live in.

The Cashmere Sweater

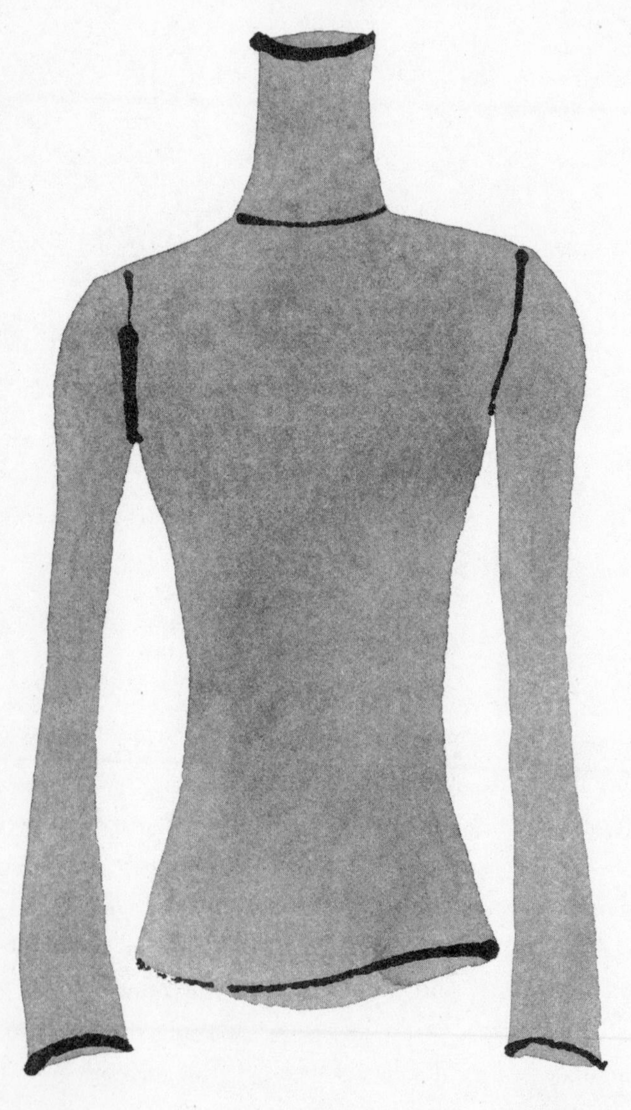

The black cashmere turtleneck is a perfect garment.

—David Mamet

IN A FAMOUS SERIES OF ADS IN THE LATE 1960S AND early 1970s, Blackglama posed the question, "What becomes a legend most?" The answer, according to Blackglama (which was a crafty adman's name for the Great Lakes Mink Association) was, naturally enough, mink. Various legends, ranging from Marlene Dietrich to Bette Davis, were recruited to pose for the ads, and draped in the most sumptuous mink coats Blackglama could produce. Though the ads were a great success, I think Blackglama got it all wrong: It isn't fur that becomes a legend most, but cashmere.

Prized since the time of the Roman Empire for its unparalleled softness, gossamer weight, and incredible warmth, cashmere is an enduring symbol of richness, both pecuniary and sensual. Just listen to what Diana Vreeland had to say when she was asked how she'd like to appear in a proposed exhibit of the twentieth century's most stylish women: "I would like to be very *luxuriously* dressed. I would like to have on the *most* luxurious black cashmere sweater, the *most* luxurious black satin pants, *very* beautiful stockings, *very* beautiful shoes—*marvelous* shoes—and whatever would be suitable around the neck."

No one understood the nuances of fashion better than this "Aztec crow" (as the model Penelope Tree described her). This was a woman who tossed off bons mots such as "Elegance is refusal," and "Pink is the navy blue of India" before breakfast. So when Diana Vreeland equated luxury with cashmere, you can be sure she knew what she was talking about. She certainly lived by her words: During her nine-year tenure as editor in chief of *Vogue* (1962–71), she wore a cashmere sweater almost every day.

I never thought very much about cashmere until perhaps six years ago, which was just about when it came into vogue again. Prior to that, I had associated it with 1950s debutantes and English matrons in tweed skirts. The term twinset made me think of shapeless garments in sad colors. *Not* my cup of tea. What turned me into a cashmere fan was an encounter with the real thing. I was writing an article about a sweater designer and went to meet her at her showroom. As we chatted, she pulled over a pile of samples for me to sift through. "Feel this. Sixteen-ply cashmere," she said, and deposited a mass of cantaloupe-colored wool in my lap. The instant my fingers touched it, I became a believer. Nothing inanimate has ever felt as lushly welcoming as that sweater. I didn't care for the color—I will never be a pastel girl—but I imagined it in black or camel and suddenly it seemed like I couldn't go on without that sweater.

What is it about cashmere that inspires such covetousness? To start with, there's the way it feels—as soft as a kiss and as warm as sunshine. When I put on my two-ply cashmere sweater—camel, ribbed, crewneck, acquired at a sample sale—I feel instantly better. It's as warm as a down comforter and as light as a feather. It wards off the chill on the darkest winter days, yet is as easy to wear as a T-shirt. It's not only gorgeous, it's hardworking.

Good quality cashmere is lush and delightfully squashy. Press your finger into it and it gives; pull the finger back and it reverts to pillowy fullness. It's so warm that some people think that it should be saved for the shivers of old age. In a piece she wrote for *The New Yorker* about the cashmere industry in Mongolia—where the bulk of the world's cashmere is gathered—Rebecca Mead quoted a fashion design instructor at the Mongolian Institute of Culture as saying, "If you wear it [cashmere] at a young age, you get used to it . . . You'd better not wear cashmere young, because when you get old you'll need even warmer things." Perhaps, though I can't imagine that anyone heeds this warning. Cashmere is much too delightful to put off.

The other quality that makes cashmere so attractive (and expensive) is its rarity. As most people know, cashmere is produced by only one type of goat, which lives in the mountains of China (where 60 percent of the world's cashmere is produced), Mongolia, and, to a much lesser degree, Afghanistan and Iran (though not, despite the name, in Kashmir). To protect them from the harsh mountain climate, these goats have both a thick, outer fleece of long hair and a downy undercoat. This downy undercoat—which, contrary to myth, grows all over the goats' bodies, not just on their bellies—is what gets spun into cashmere mufflers and cardigans. Once a year, these goats are wrestled to the ground by nomadic cashmere herders, their shaggy outer fur is parted, and the soft down that grows underneath teased off with large iron combs. Even the most enthusiastic cashmere gatherer can't get more than 2.6 ounces to 3.4 ounces from each goat—and that's after the long hairs, grease, dirt, and dried feces are separated out from the good stuff. Since it takes at least 8.8 ounces of cashmere to make a woman's sweater, this works out to a third of a sweater per goat—more for men's sweaters and large items such as blankets. A herd of one hundred goats can produce maybe 22 pounds of cashmere a year. So there you have it—a concentrated area of production combined with a limited amount of raw product. Not surprisingly, cashmere has been a habit of wealth.

This, however, is changing. While it is certainly still possible to buy a $2,600 cashmere pullover, companies such as Banana Republic and J. Crew have put cashmere onto the backs of those willing to part with as little as $89.99. There is a difference between a four-figure cashmere sweater and a two-figure one, of course, just as there is a difference between a Rolls Royce and a Ford Neon. Both will get you where you want to go, but only one will do so with style to spare. The best cashmere is made of fibers that are fine and long: far narrower than a human hair in circumference and about 1.5 inches in length. Long, fine hairs are not only warmer, they are less likely to pill. The short, thick ones, on the other hand, are not nearly as warm, and will pill after a few wearings. So if a cashmere sweater seems like an unbelievable bargain, rest assured that it is.

The conditions that made the $89.99 cashmere sweater possible provide a lesson in the perils of capitalism. For most of the twentieth century, Mongolia was part of the Soviet Union, and so didn't participate in the world economy. Mongolian cashmere herders sold their crop to the state, which set quotas for the number of goats each herder could have and determined the price of raw cashmere. Mongolian cashmere was used to produce sweaters for the Eastern European market. With the fall of Communism and the subsequent switch over to a free-market system, Mongolian herders, who had once received a salary from the state, were left to fend for themselves. Most have fewer than one hundred goats, which keeps the return on their investment low. Because they were paid by volume, many of these now impoverished herders crossbred their cashmere goats with angora goats, which have coarser hair. Production skyrocketed, while quality declined. In China, loosening of market controls led to much the same situation. Moreover, because China is not a member of the Cashmere & Camel Hair Manufacturers Institute, which regulates cashmere quality, Chinese cashmere, which tends to be thicker and shorter than Mongolian cashmere, is often blended with yak hair, merino wool, or nylon. At the same time that the Mongolians and the Chinese were ramping up their cashmere production, the Japanese economy cooled. What had once been a major source of revenue for the Chinese suddenly dried up, and they were left with warehouses full of unsold goods. The result: a world glut of cashmere, much of it of indifferent quality.

Back in the United States, this has meant that the cashmere sweater, once a status symbol that was out of the reach of all but a very few, is ubiquitous. In the fall of 1999, for example, Banana Republic's entire ad campaign was built around cashmere. That same year, Gap began selling cashmere for babies. You can now buy cashmere at Target. Even QVC, the home shopping network, hawks cashmere. This is a far cry from cashmere's one-time association with debutantes and rich girls. As one woman told Ellen Melinkoff about her high school in the 1950s: "There was a real snob sweater hierarchy . . . A cashmere or lambs' wool or angora set, the height of chic, was simply unattainable to most high school girls." In Eisenhower's America, a cashmere sweater was something that every woman aspired to. Unlike more esoteric, Old World, and rarely seen status symbols, such as an Hermès Kelly bag or a Balenciaga suit, a cashmere sweater set was as solid and admirable as a Cadillac—just the thing to wear with pearls. In terms of fashion, those were relatively unsophisticated times. Today, we like our status symbols to be a little harder to come by; women whose mothers yearned for cashmere sweaters in high school now think nothing of putting their names on the waiting list for a pricey Hermès bag.

In the novel *The Black Dahlia,* set in the late 1940s, James Ellroy describes Kay Lake, a former prostitute, as "South Dakota white trash molded by a cop's love." As a police detective's paramour, Kay reads widely, studies art, and listens to Schubert. But the hard evidence of how far she's come in the world sits in a glass-fronted mahogany cabinet in her living room: "It was filled with Kay's cashmere sweaters, all the shades of the rainbow at forty dollars a pop." At a time when the average salary was three thousand dollars a year, this was no small feat.

As Americans became more prosperous and cashmere sweaters became less rare, a cashmere sweater with a history became more prestigious than one fresh from Henri Bendel. In 1980, Judith Krantz, whose fashion sense is unerring, describes just such a sweater in *Princess Daisy*. In the scene, Daisy is helping her best friend, usually an unorthodox dresser, prepare for her first meeting with her boyfriend's socially important family. "'Here's a heavy sweater you can borrow—you don't own a decent fall coat.' 'A white cashmere cardigan? Daisy, that's from before we went to college, it's from when you were a kid in London!' 'Anyone can buy a sweater, but ancient, definitely yellowing cashmere—they'll understand that.'"

Cashmere was prized long before it was made into sweaters, however. It was sporadically fashionable in Europe, most notably in the early nineteenth century, when Napoleon's victorious troops brought cashmere shawls they had taken from vanquished Egyptian warriors. Though the oblong shawls had been worn by men in the Middle East, the

French thought them rather feminine, and presented them to their wives and sweethearts. (Napoleon himself gave seventeen to his wife.) Finer and warmer than anything then available in Europe, where the production of cashmere was unknown, the shawls caused a sensation that soon spread across the continent. Known as ring shawls because, despite their generous size, they were fine enough to be pulled through a wedding ring, these fabulously expensive accessories became the centerpiece of every fashionable woman's wardrobe. Jean-Auguste-Dominique Ingres, a painter with the eye of a fashion editor, made frequent use of these shawls in his portraiture. *Marie-Françoise Beauregard, Mme. Rivière,* painted in 1806, depicts the wife of an ambitious civil servant. She's propped on a blue plush sofa, and encircled by a cream-colored cashmere shawl with a narrow woven pattern in reds and greens down the side, and a deep border in what was known as the pinecone motif. Mme. Rivière's shawl was very likely one of her most prized possessions, for it marked her as a woman of taste. (Likewise, her ability to drape and maneuver it to perfection was a sign of her grace.) As the *Journal de Paris* reported in 1805, "the elegance of a woman can be equated with the quality of her shawl, or rather, its price." However, their popularity was probably not based solely on aesthetics—to the women of the early nineteenth century, shivering in their skimpy, neoclassical fashions, these cozy wraps must have seemed a godsend.

Cashmere was also a popular dressmaking fabric for much of the nineteenth century. In black, it was considered a safe and subdued choice—perfect for, say, governesses, who had to negotiate the tricky no-woman's-land of being not quite guests and not quite servants. Laura Ingalls Wilder, the pioneer heroine who turned her life story into a series of books about growing up on the frontier of a young country, was married in a black cashmere dress. She was making one as part of her trousseau, because her mother thought that every married woman should have a black dress and considered cashmere a good, serviceable fabric. When the weddings plans were unexpectedly moved up, Laura wore her newly finished best dress.

Laura's dress was not, obviously, a stretchy knit; it was cut from woven fabric. Though it's still used this way for coats and suits, to many people cashmere means just one thing: sweaters. However, the sweater wasn't developed until the end of the nineteenth century, and even then, it was worn only by male athletes. The idea was that a knitted woolen garment would help athletes work up a good sweat—then considered healthy. Thus the unlovely origin of the term sweater.

There were a few bulky, jacket-style cardigans made for women before World War I, but they weren't especially stylish. Coco Chanel was an early sweater fan. Though the Chanel myth is so towering that it's hard to tell what's true and what isn't, legend has it that one chilly day on the polo field, Chanel borrowed one of the player's jerseys, belted it, and found it to her liking. She began to make and sell similar sweaters at her shop in Deauville, where they were snapped up by discriminating customers. But women at large didn't start wearing sweaters until 1918, when, after four years of knitting socks, balaclavas, and mufflers for the men off fighting the war, they decided to make things for themselves.

In the 1920s, fashion relaxed considerably, and the sweater really hit its stride. Hand-knitted sweaters had a vogue, but the time it took to make one meant that most women preferred to buy one ready-made. Pringle of Scotland, a firm that had been making socks and underwear since 1815, saw an opportunity, and turned its attention to sweaters, chiefly of cashmere. Within a few years, Pringle became known as one of the world's best cashmere sweater makers. The designer Elsa Schiaparelli, who later became known for her surrealist-inspired suits and dresses, began her career in 1928 with a hand-knitted trompe l'oeil sweater. It was black, with a faux white bow and shawl collar.

The fashionable sweater of the period was V-necked, loose, and came down over the hips—just the thing to wear over the boyishly flat figure that was considered ideal at the time. Unlike the high-necked blouses that had preceded it, the sweater was comfortable, casual, and sporty. At first, it was worn mainly for sports and other informal events. But once women experienced the comfort of sportswear, they began to wear it on other occasions. Both physically and psychologically, sportswear is freer than more formal types of clothing. As social mores became less stringent, people instinctively wanted to dress down rather than up. In *The Sun Also Rises,* Ernest Hemingway describes Lady Brett Ashley as follows: "She wore a slipover jersey and a tweed skirt, and her hair was brushed back like a boy's. She started all that." What is interesting about this passage is not that Brett is wearing a pullover and a skirt, but where she is wearing this outfit: She's at a bar in Paris. Women had been wearing sweaters to play golf or tennis for several years, but the idea of wearing a sweater out for a drink was novel. Nowadays, we wouldn't think twice about doing so. At the time, however, Brett was a trendsetter.

For those who have the style to pull it off, the sweater and skirt look can be incredibly elegant. Of Gloria Guinness, whose mysterious origins—she was rumored to be the illegitimate daughter of a laundress—didn't prevent her from claiming a place on the Best-Dressed list, John Fairchild wrote, in *Chic Savages,* "La Guinness was the chicest of all in a black cardigan and black skirt." He was referring to her pre-World War II days in Paris, before she made the first of her fortuitous marriages. Even when Gloria was penniless, she managed to make an impression.

In the 1930s, figures rounded, and the sweater shrank to better define curves. The fit wasn't tight, at least at first, but it was more body conscious. The biggest development of the decade was the introduction of the twinset—a short-sleeve pullover worn with a matching, long-sleeve cardigan, for which Pringle claims responsibility. An ad for a sweater manufacturer called H.A.&E. Smith in the July 15, 1934, issue of *Vogue* gives an idea of how unexpected this idea seemed: "Now isn't that just like a woman?" reads the copy. "To have a perfectly good sweater and then go and put another on top of it? Oh well, everyone's doing it, and our guess is that it's because both sweaters are so soft, so good-looking, that they can't be resisted. Indian Cashmere, in beautiful pastel shades." The twinset became especially associated with coeds, who collected them in every color. This made the late 1930s rise of the Sweater Girl doubly enticing: As epitomized by the busty Lana Turner, the Sweater Girl wore the same crewneck pullover that wholesome college girls did—except hers was skintight.

The movie that established Turner as the Sweater Girl was her first, the presciently titled *They Won't Forget.* Her screen time was brief yet memorable: She played a sexy schoolgirl, and all she did was walk down the street of a small southern town. That was enough. At the preview, the male high school and college students in the audience whooped and hollered, and a starlet was born. According to *The Films of Lana Turner,* by Lou Valentino, "Lana's brief appearance in *They Won't Forget* made an impact not only on her but on the sweater industry. Lana brought sweaters into vogue. Every American girl built her wardrobe around them." Valentino adds that one observer claimed "More sheep were shorn for wool in the years that followed than in all history, for sweaters became the rage."

The sweater was a practical necessity during WWII, when public spaces were apt to be unheated. They were worn under jackets or with skirts or slacks, and very often had padded shoulders, to create the widely worn broad shoulder look. Diana Vreeland, then a fashion editor at *Harper's Bazaar,* popularized (among other things) the turtleneck sweater, another one of today's basics that only *seems* to have been around and classic forever.

The New Look of the late 1940s pushed aside the informality of sweaters, at least for those who aspired to high fashion. With his wasp waists and full skirts, Christian Dior liked blouses or coordinating suit jackets (which were often so fitted that nothing could be worn under them). But for many American women—not just high school girls—the sweater remained a staple. The sweater-and-skirt approach to dress reached its zenith in C.Z. Guest, the simply attired socialite who was one of Truman Capote's Swans. "I remember seeing C.Z. once in Paris, in the fifties," reminisced Bill Blass in his memoir, *Bare Blass*. "She came into the bar of the Ritz wearing a knee-length tweed skirt, a twinset, and moccasins—and in a time when everyone was tarted up in Dior's New Look, she stopped traffic." Perhaps it was this nonchalant elegance that Blass had in mind when he designed an evening ensemble of a taffeta ball skirt and a long cashmere cardigan. This ensemble is now a classic American look.

But the sweater wasn't accepted everywhere: In her biography, *In and Out of Vogue* former *Vogue* editor in chief Grace Mirabella relates that in the 1950s she lost a job because she showed up in a sweater—a chic Italian sweater, to be sure, but apparently not the thing for a rising young fashion editor to be seen in.

By the early 1960s, the cashmere sweater's status was unassailable. It was dependable, classic, and, above all else, safe—admirable qualities, but ones that were completely at odds with the daring fashion of the 1960s. Many women kept right on wearing cashmere twinsets and tweed skirts, but they were outside the "in" crowd. The signature sweater of the 1960s was the poor boy, a ribbed pullover with a body-hugging fit. The idea was to pull it down hard and tuck it into your miniskirt. The poor boy was made in a variety of knits, but I doubt that cashmere was among them. In the 1960s, cashmere and fashion went their separate ways. Those who followed fashion considered cashmere stodgy and dull—something a maiden aunt would wear. Those who carried on wearing cashmere thought fashion had disintegrated to a pitiful state. It wasn't until Halston began using cashmere in the early 1970s that it regained its fashionable reputation.

Roy Halston Frowick, better known by his middle name alone, took classic American sportswear—shirtwaist dresses, knits, pants—and transformed them into high fashion. He did this by reimaginging these simple separates in the most luxurious fabrics he could find, including cashmere. Halston made twinsets, but they fit much closer to the body than anything coming out of the Scottish mills, and they were as likely to fasten with a zipper as with dyed-to-match buttons. Halston demystified cashmere by using it in unconventional ways: He made long, hooded evening dresses out of it, as well as loose pants, bodysuits, caftans, hooded pullovers, and polo-neck dresses. When Grace Mirabella, newly named to the top post at *Vogue,* went to Paris to cover the couture shows in 1971, she took with her an entire wardrobe of Halston mix 'n' match cashmere separates. To her more fussily dressed European colleagues, who were unaccustomed to Halston's understated luxe, Mirabella looked, as the *International Herald Tribune* reported, "like the girl next door" in her "sweater." This wasn't meant as a compliment. Even some American women were surprised to find that

Halston's cashmere knits were so chic. In *Halston: An American Original,* the fashion editor Ellin Saltzman is quoted as saying of the designer: "Nobody had ever shown me before that you could get dressed up and look elegant in a cashmere sweater."

But the innate elegance of Halston's vision eventually won over the fashion world, and today he is considered an industry giant. Yet by the mid-1980s, when Halston faded from the scene, cashmere had once again receded into the fashion netherworld of boring staples. Mass-market sportswear manufacturers such as J. Crew offered preppy styles at affordable prices, and high-end Scottish mills continued to turn out very predictable and very expensive sweater sets. It wasn't until TSE launched its line of updated cashmere knits, in 1989, that cashmere was again seen as a stylish fabric. "Basically, cashmere was overpriced and precious. We wanted to move beyond folded cashmere cardigans. Cashmere doesn't have to be a sweater. It can be a whole outfit. You can wear it to the office, to bed . . . even out at night," Rebecca Shafer, one of the line's founders, told *Vogue* in December 1992. TSE moved cashmere back into the fashion sphere by dying it offbeat colors (what *Vogue* described as "hard-to-find chalky shades of lavender, peridot, indigo, and sand") and knitting it into nonstodgy shapes: tank tops, hoodies, poor-boy turtlenecks, and T-shirts. Moreover, TSE's prices were reasonable—a classic bulky turtleneck cost about $270—which made cashmere available to a new generation of consumers. By 1999, TSE was doing $60 million a year in business in the United States.

As the '90s progressed, cashmere's fashion value grew by leaps and bounds. It seemed like every designer in the world was making cashmere sweaters, some of them very far from the twinset ideal—Marc Jacobs made one that looked like thermal underwear. Priced at more than $800, it made the cover of *Vogue.* As Rebecca Mead wrote in *The New Yorker* in February 1999: "The fabric's understated luxury is well suited to a cultural moment in which unshowy self-indulgence is the highest ideal—a moment when a perfectly tailored but unobtrusive Jil Sander suit is better than a gold-buttoned Chanel two-piece." In other words, cashmere is a subtle indulgence. It doesn't announce itself; instead you have to know enough to recognize it.

Today, cashmere is an all-purpose basic. In fact, in the July 2002 issue of *Harper's Bazaar,* which was devoted to dressing well at every age, cashmere appeared on women of all ages. Of course, there are ways to make even a staple exclusive. One way to do this with cashmere is to wear it when its vaunted warmth is completely superfluous, even a drawback—in the summertime, for instance. Interviewed by *Vanity Fair* in September 2000, the designer Michael Kors described seeing a woman in a cashmere dress in August. "I said, 'Aren't you roasting?' She said, 'Cashmere is seasonless.' To me, nothing is more fabulous than women who don't have to deal with the elements."

Most women, however, do have to deal with the elements, and would find a cashmere sundress about as useful as a gingham windbreaker. For those of us—I count myself among them—who need warmth in the winter, not the summer, I say get a cashmere turtleneck. Something very thin, black, with high armholes, and a close fit around the neck. Such a sweater will make you feel elegant, swanlike, and chic—as well as nonchalant and comfortable. A ball gown might transform you into a queen for a night, but a black cashmere turtleneck allows you to look regal every day. It truly is, as David Mamet said, a perfect garment.

The White Shirt

A white-shirt woman is a busy, inspired person . . . I think of Kate Hepburn as a white-shirt woman. I think of Audrey Hepburn. Mrs. Vreeland and Jackie O., definitely. Marilyn Monroe, definitely not.

—Isaac Mizrahi

EVERY ONCE IN A WHILE, AS I'M FLIPPING THROUGH a fashion magazine, I'll come across a feature on dressing according to your astrological sign. I always chuckle at what I, as a Leo, am supposed to feel most like myself in, because the editors invariably suggest such attention-grabbing gambits as sheer, leopard-print shirts, clingy orange tops, and slit-to-there purple skirts—the kind of look-at-me clothes I instinctively recoil from. My inner Vegas showgirl, if she exists, has never nudged me toward such flamboyant plumage. Instead, I spend a lot of my time in jeans and denim skirts. In the winter, I pair these twin lynchpins of my wardrobe with a succession of black sweaters. In the summer, I like to wear some sort of white shirt. It can be a tunic, a preppy button-down, or a plain old T-shirt—as long as it's white cotton, I feel (or at least appear) cool and fresh no matter how hot it gets.

Of course, air-conditioning and relaxed dress codes have broadened summer wardrobe options considerably. Hot-weather clothes no longer have to be light—in both senses of the word—to be bearable. But after several summers of seeing more bra straps and midriffs than I care to remember, I have renewed admiration for the white shirt, a garment so intrinsically stylish that at least one designer—Anne Fontaine—produces little else.

Many of the women whose style I admire were photographed in white shirts. Slim Keith liked to pair them with black trousers and a red bolero for evening. This was in the 1940s, when most of her contemporaries didn't feel dressed for dinner unless they were in beaded crepe gowns with shoulders out to there and major jewels. Jane Birkin seemed invariably to be wearing a clingy white T and faded jeans, a basket in her hand and little heels on her tanned feet. Before her transformation into grown-up perfection at the hands of Hubert de Givenchy, Audrey Hepburn improvised a chic, gamine look; one of her frequent tricks was to wear an oversized man's white shirt, the tails wrapped twice around her tiny waist. But the white shirt image that remains the most vivid to me is that of an anonymous young woman shot on the street in New York by a *Life* photographer in the late 1960s. Her white shirt is tucked into an A-line skirt that bares her legs. Her brown hair is long and shiny, and she's striding purposefully along in flat sandals, as though she's on her way somewhere she both needs and wants to be. I only saw this photo once, years ago, but the woman's direct, lean style has had a strong influence on my taste. I was reminded of it when I read a remark Polly Allen Mellen made in *Harper's Bazaar* about Carolyn Bessette Kennedy: "She was so American: her nonchalant attitude, the way she put on a white T-shirt and jeans."

The white shirt is a centerpiece of American style, as much as blue jeans are. White shirts are worn by women all over the world, yes, but it's the attitude of a white shirt that makes it so quintessentially American. For its one-hundredth anniversary, in April 1992, the American edition of *Vogue* put ten of that year's top models on the cover—all in white shirts. The white shirt speaks of a roll-up-your-sleeves briskness, a directness that has no time for fussy details or nonfunctional flourishes. It's impractical color gives it an aristocratic flair, while its ready availability makes it a mass favorite. It's the best of both worlds for consumers of all income brackets—and what's more American than that?

In cotton, silk, or linen, worn in the daytime with jeans or in the evening with a long, black skirt—as a radiant Ali MacGraw did at the 2001 Academy Awards—the white shirt is unpretentious, fresh, and naturally refined. It represents both simplicity and a fresh, well-scrubbed sensibility—what Truman Capote called "a soap and lemon cleanness."

The purest form of the white shirt is the white T-shirt, a garment Giorgio Armani described in Alice Harris's *The White T* as "the Alpha and the Omega of the fashion alphabet. The creative universe begins with its essentiality, and whatever path the imagination takes, ends with its purity." Adapted by women in the 1960s, and since improved by any number of designers—notably Agnès B., who has made refining the basic elements of dress into an art form—the white T-shirt is both luxurious and down-to-earth. Even the most discriminating consumers seem to agree on this point: For its September 2002 issue, *Vogue* asked various fashion types what they would buy if they had one thousand dollars to spend. Cameron Silver, the owner of Decades, one of the best vintage boutiques in the United States and a man who could buy pretty much any outfit he wanted, answered, "$500 in white cotton Hanro classic T-shirts—and $500 to charity: that way it's a win-win situation." Giorgio Armani, who is a self-confessed T-shirt addict (what better to set off his permanent tan?) said much the same thing ten years earlier, when *Vogue* asked him and several other members of the chic set to define luxury (no price limit on this one). "Luxury," said Armani, "is a white T-shirt, absolutely clean, with diamond bracelets going all the way up a brown arm."

That anyone can march into a Gap—where Bessette Kennedy was rumored to have bought hers—and pick out a white shirt is a small triumph of democracy. Gap is a great equalizer in that it lets noncelebrities dress like celebrities—a point that the company underscored by photographing both the famous and the unknown in its signature white pocket T-shirt for its breakthrough 1989 ad campaign. The crisp, black-and-white photos gave each subject a burnished, iconographic stateliness—and catapulted Gap into the front ranks of fashion.

Both literally and symbolically, white is the most easily sullied of colors. In its pristine state, it connotes purity and innocence; marred by so much as a single smudge, it seems irrevocably soiled. Perhaps because it is so difficult to maintain the integrity of white, literary heroines who are doomed to a bad end are often first introduced in white. Daisy Miller, the willful, impetuous title character of Henry James's 1878 short story, makes her debut as a vision of American innocence abroad: "She was dressed in white muslin, with a hundred frills and flounces and knots of pale-colored ribbon. Bareheaded, she balanced in her hand a large parasol with a deep border of embroidery; and she was strikingly, admirably pretty." Within weeks, Daisy is dead of "Roman fever," brought on, it is speculated, by unchaperoned moonlight drives through malarial Rome with an Italian guide. Since her behavior was unorthodox by contemporary standards, her downfall is as much moral as it is physiological. She couldn't live up to her white raiment.

In Christianity, white is the color of heavenly perfection. In Christian art, God the father and his angels wear white robes; in real life, the Pope does, as do some orders of nuns, altar boys (and, now, girls), and girls making their First Communions.

White is also, of course, the color of modern Western wedding dresses. Though Queen Victoria's orange-blossom trimmed white satin wedding dress of 1840 sparked a trend among the upper classes, most middle- and working-class women kept on getting married in whatever color looked prettiest on them. Women of all classes continued to wear their wedding gowns as best dresses. For brides with limited incomes, this was a practical necessity; among the wealthy it was thought quite charming for a new wife to appear at the opera or a dinner wearing her wedding dress (made over to reveal her shoulders and arms, as was considered appropriate for a married woman in the evening). In Edith Wharton's novel *The Age of Innocence*, this custom provides a metaphor for the disintegrating relationship of Newland and May Archer. The evening on which Archer plans to tell May that he intends to leave her for Ellen Olenska, May wears her wedding dress, which is accidentally splashed with filth from the gutter as she alights from their carriage. Before Archer can speak his piece, May informs him that Ellen is going to live in Europe. Archer then realizes that he is tied to a wife he doesn't love for the rest of his life. As he watches, May leaves the room, "her torn and muddy wedding dress dragging after her."

It wasn't until the 1920s that the white wedding became standard. Just as women began making inroads into professions that valued intelligence and talent over virginity, the traditional symbol of maidenhood became de rigueur. This was also the time when wedding gowns ceased to look like fashionable, albeit white, dresses and began to resemble archaic costumes, with trains, fitted bodices, and full skirts. The role of virgin that a woman assumed on her wedding day was just that, a role to be played for the duration of the ceremony. The next day, wearing ordinary clothes was resumed.

White is always a little out of the ordinary. It lends an air of untouchability—a woman who dresses all in white tends to come across as fragile and delicate as a gardenia. A man dressed in white, on the other hand, seems eccentric. Author Tom Wolfe, who affects archaically tailored white suits, is a prime example of this sort of idiosyncrasy: In photos, he always resembles a visitor from a more genteel era. Indeed, white clothes and privilege go hand in hand, because in order for a garment to stay white, its wearer must abstain from activities that might cause it to become dirty. Because white is so impractical, choosing to wear it implies a degree of elitism. If you wear white, you have to be prepared for the upkeep. Every winter I gaze longingly at white wool coats, and every winter I sternly remind myself of the dry-cleaning bills that such a purchase would incur. In the nineteenth century, when antiperspirants and dry cleaners were nonexistent and doing laundry involved considerably more work than tossing a load into the machine and remembering to add fabric softener, ladies and gentlemen were known by their clean, white personal linen. Unlike the working classes, they could afford to wear fresh underwear and shirts everyday; it was one of the marks of their high status. Even today, we refer to white-collar and blue-collar jobs; the former suggests desk work in a well-ventilated office, the latter, something involving manual labor and perspiration. The catch, explains Alison Lurie in *The Language of Clothes*, is this: "The easily soiled white or pale-colored shirt that signifies freedom from manual labor is in constant danger of embarrassing its wearer with grimy cuffs or ring around the collar." So while wearing white is a privilege, it is also a responsibility.

The modern white shirt is adapted from men's underwear, which may explain why the sight of a woman wearing nothing but her lover's white shirt, as Annette Bening did in *The American President*, has such an erotic charge. Until the very late eighteenth century, men's shirts weren't supposed to show; they were worn as a layer between the body and the outer garment. Women wore chemises, or shifts, that served the same purpose. The idea was that this garment could be more easily and frequently laundered—relatively speaking—than a dress or a jacket, which, in the case of the upper classes, could often not be cleaned at all because of the profusion of embroidery and other embellishments. (This dress strategy was not exclusive to the West: In Japan, the most delicate kimonos could not be cleaned and were worn over simpler robes as a protective measure.) A plain white chemise might peek out from the neckline of a dress, but it was very much an undergarment.

Once men adopted the simple and sober suit and shirt uniform, by the end of the nineteenth century, cleanliness of a shirt took on a new importance. Shirt fronts and cuffs were on display, and a new stress on cleanliness required that they be faultlessly white. The chief proponent of the new cult of personal hygiene was George Brummell, known as Beau because of his devotion to elegance. Brummell was one of the first Europeans in a thousand years to endorse a daily immersion in water—as part of his daily toilette, he also soaked in a tub of milk to keep his skin soft—rather than the energetic application of scent onto unbathed flesh. Because of his friendship with the Prince of Wales, Brummell's habits were picked up by the fashionable world. A true original and an unmitigated snob, Brummell also pioneered short hair for men, clean-shaven chins, and a nearly rabid pursuit of expensive simplicity. One of his signature motifs was a precisely knotted, blindingly white cravat. Made of a square of starched muslin the size of a large napkin, the cravat was the equivalent of a modern necktie, in that it protruded above the tightly buttoned jackets that men wore at the time.

Brummell would spend hours perfecting the knotting of his cravat. One morning visitor, on inquiring about the small mountain of snowy linen on the floor of Brummell's dressing room, was mournfully informed by the dandy's valet, "Those are our failures." For Brummell, a wrinkle was enough to mar the perfection of his whites.

Though few went to the extremes Brummell did, clean linen did become one of the hallmarks of a gentle birth and good fortune. (And a standard that budding aristocrats still emulate: When she was first lady, Jacqueline Kennedy reputedly had her bed linen changed after every use—even after her afternoon nap.) But for women, white shifts and petticoats still remained under wraps. Since dresses were made in one piece, it wasn't until the suit became popular, in the 1880s, that the shirtwaist, as shirts were known, became necessary. By the turn of the twentieth century, the cotton shirtwaist was a key component of American women's wardrobes, the ideal accompaniment to the flared skirt that was then the height of style. According to Caroline Rennolds Milbank, the author of *New York Fashion*, "American women loved the practicality of shirtwaists, which were easy to launder . . . and they resisted attempts by couturiers to introduce blouses, of silk or other materials."

The high-collared, low-breasted shirtwaist was a favorite of the Gibson Girl, the idealized symbol of American womanhood drawn by Charles Dana Gibson and epitomized by his wife, Irene Langhorne. Tall, statuesque, and crowned with a towering pompadour, the Gibson Girl represented the modern, active woman of 1890 to 1910. She was modish and attractive, but in a brisk, thoroughly New World way—the

Gibson Girl was more likely to beat her man at tennis than sit languorously on the sidelines applauding his victory. The no-nonsense but still feminine shirtwaist was her preferred garb—and for the millions of American women who wanted to look like her, it was an easily obtained item. Like the suit, the shirtwaist was a fairly democratic fashion. Its price rose with the addition of luxuries such as handmade lace, but for the most part the shirtwaist was easy to mass produce, and could be bought quite cheaply.

The most potent permutation of white-shirt innocence was the version worn by schoolgirls. In *Gilded City: Scandal and Sensation in Turn-of-the-Century New York*, M. H. Dunlop describes how the schoolgirl—young, naive, virginal—was a sexual turn-on for many men. One woman he quotes describes how, when she was attending the Brearley School, on the Upper East Side of Manhattan in the 1890s, "All the gentlemen from the Union Club, anchored next to the Cathedral, knew the pretty school girls by sight, and the pretty school girls knew them." When Edith Nesbitt, a former showgirl and one of the sexual icons of the Edwardian age, took the stand at her husband's 1906 trial for the murder of architect Stanford White, Nesbitt's former lover, she shrewdly wore a demure white shirtwaist. Dunlop writes, "She asserted visible innocence for the benefit of the innocent segment of the public and she sought to arouse any man present who found the schoolgirl look to be sexually exciting." This still holds true: the white shirt, along with the short, pleated skirt, and kneesocks of the stereotypical schoolgirl are a persistent pornographic prop.

Where the schoolgirl's white middy blouse differed from the shirtwaist worn by grown women was in its lack of adornment. Edwardian high style called for all-out embellishment. Pin tucks, lace inserts, lace trim, and embroidery were rampant. The labor involved in constructing these fragile concoctions was considerable. In volume one of her memoir, *The Rainbow Comes and Goes*, Lady Diana Cooper, one of the most renowned hostesses of her day, recalled that in the early years of the twentieth century, her German governess spent two years making an elaborate, lace-encrusted shirtwaist.

One of the first women to recognize the appeal of the plain, white, schoolgirl-style shirt was Coco Chanel. She was probably drawn to its plainness because it was so different from what other women wore, and Coco always strove to make herself unique. As she was far from the ideal Belle Epoque beauty, being skinny and dark rather than plump and rosy, the wedding-cake styles of the time didn't suit her. Chanel found she looked best in simple, menswear-inspired clothes, and she was smart enough to exploit her discovery. When other women saw how fetching these radically pared-down garments looked, they, too, wanted to wear them. Paired with the simplified suits of the war years, the plain white shirt became a hallmark of the new way of dressing. By the late teens, the lace and flounces of the Edwardian age were regarded as old-fashioned.

The classic white shirt of the 1920s was the middy, a loose-fitting, sailor-style blouse that was gathered into a wide band which sat on the hips. It was a sporty, casual look, and like many '20s fashions, it was adapted from children's clothing. It was worn for playing tennis and golf; slightly fancier versions were considered appropriate with suits. Along with pleated skirts, cloche hats, and T-strap shoes, the middy is one of the most easily recognized of that decade's fashions. A photo taken by Edward Steichen and published in *Vogue* on July 15, 1928, typifies the blouse-and-skirt dressing of the age. Three women are sitting on what appears to be the deck of a yacht. All are looking off to the right, and one is using binoculars, suggesting that they are observing some sort of sporting event (a favorite pastime of models in 1920s fashion photos and illustrations). They are dressed in the easy blazers, skirts, and blouses of the period; all three faces are partially obscured by close-fitting hats. The woman on the right is clad in a white middy, a white pleated skirt that just brushes her knees, and what appears to be a linen jacket. Her legs are flapper slender, and she wears a pearl choker. She is the epitome of the '20s sportswoman.

The '20s also saw the birth of the *garçonne* look, named for Victor Margueritte's 1922 novel, *La Garçonne,* about a sexually liberated Sorbonne student who cuts her hair short and wears a man's shirt, suit, and tie. Though few women adopted the *garçonne* style head-to-toe, the fashion of wearing a white shirt and necktie was widespread. In 1926, the year when skirts were at their shortest and the sportswear craze at its peak, the unfashionable couldn't "tell the boys from the girls," writes Georgina Howell in *In Vogue*. The shirt-and-tie look eventually came to be associated with the intellectual women of the Bloomsbury set. In Dorothy L. Sayers's much-loved mystery novels about the aristocratic sleuth Lord Peter

Wimsey, Lord Peter's paramour, Harriet Vane—novelist, Oxford graduate, and bonafide Bloomsbury resident—is a devotee of the look.

The next time the white shirt made a significant impact on fashion was in the late 1940s, when bobby-soxers began wearing their fathers' cast-off dress shirts with their jeans. Though frequently criticized by adults for being sloppy, the look was a favorite of teenage girls, and was popular into the 1950s. Ellen Melinkoff calls the oversized man's shirt the era's "respite from fit and neatness." But it was only worn for the most casual of activities: "to wash the dishes, the dog, the car." For any other activity, the 1950s white shirt of choice was darted, starched, and ironed to crisp perfection. The teenage ideal, according to Melinkoff, was made by Ship 'n Shore: "These blouses typified the fifties sporty look—the finely pointed collar turned up to complement an Italian haircut, maybe even with a button open at the neck. We might fill in the neck with a garrote-tied scarf." But though "the working class dream was a closet filled with Ship 'n Shore tops," that dream came at a no small cost: "A $2.98 Ship 'n Shore white blouse was still a status symbol to us in the fifties by virtue of the labor it took to keep it washed, starched, and pressed. Most Ship 'n Shores probably spent half their lives in the vegetable bins of refrigerators, damp and waiting for the iron." The era's high-end version of the perfect white shirt was the Bettina blouse, made by Hubert de Givenchy for his first collection in 1952, and named for the model who wore it. With its convertible collar and full, ruffle-covered sleeves, the Bettina was doubtless far more daunting an ironing project than the relatively simple Ship 'n Shores. But then, a woman who could afford Givenchy probably had someone else doing her laundry. Unless, of course, she was Babe Paley, the patrician beauty who spent years on the Best-Dressed list: Despite the considerable wealth she enjoyed as the wife of Bill Paley, Babe would wash and press her heavy white piqué cotton shirts herself, because she didn't want to ask anyone else to take on such an unpleasant task.

The fresh, youthful appeal of the white shirt assured its crossover into the styles of the 1960s. Early in the decade, designers such as Mary Quant played with its schoolgirl appeal by pairing it with the tiniest of jumpers and flat Mary Janes. François Truffaut's 1961 film *Jules et Jim*, starring Jeanne Moreau and set in the early years of the century, epitomized this trend. In it, Moreau sported vaguely retro, vaguely modern getups that centered on plain white shirts worn with vests, newsboy caps, and knickerbockers—a look that had a huge impact on young fashion. Four years later, Moreau appeared alongside Brigitte Bardot in another influential white-shirt film: Louis Malle's comic western, *Viva Maria!* It's also set soon after the turn of the twentieth century, but its heroines wear the high-collared, ruffled blouses of stereotypical frontier schoolmarms. This look, too, translated into a widespread craze for romantic styles, including lace-up granny boots, shawls, velvet ribbons, and floor-sweeping skirts, that lasted into the early 1970s. Shops such as Mexicana in London even sold lacy white bloomers—what a turn-of-the-century belle would have worn under her skirt and petticoats—as outerwear. As Ellen Melinkoff notes, the granny look "seemed to express our back-to-nature, return-to-a-simpler-time, antiplastic yearnings. We needed some assurance that the world wasn't changing too fast. For comfort we turned to home-baked bread, macramé, and Laura Ashley dresses."

The appeal of heading off to the office dressed like a milkmaid eventually paled. By 1973, designers were referencing the fluid lines of 1930s sportswear, which included unadorned white shirts, often worn under wool pullovers or vests. In 1977, Diane Keaton, in *Annie Hall,* loosened this look up by wearing the shirt and vest several sizes too large, and adding a kooky hat and cowboy boots. When John T. Molloy wrote *The Woman's Dress for Success Book* in the same year, he "tested" various blouse colors to see which would give a woman the most authority in the workplace. White came out on top, with pale yellow, pale beige, ecru, and beige following. At the bottom of the list were such objectionable shades as kelly green, gold, and salmon. Not surprising, really. Male executives had worn white shirts for generations, and they took respect for granted. Just like men, women were supposed to wear white shirts and dark suits. It was enough to give the white shirt a bad name, which is probably why many women turned to brighter colored blouses in the 1980s. The white shirt still symbolized patrician good taste in 1988, however: When Melanie Griffith made the leap from the secretarial pool to the corner office in *Working Girl,* she traded her gaudy lower-class prints for a white shirt and a dark suit.

The early '90s were a big white-shirt time, in part because companies such as Gap and J.Crew made back-to-basics dressing both sexy and stylish. One of the decade's most imitated films, *Pulp Fiction,* featured a white-shirt-wearing heroine in a classic bob (Uma Thurman). The white shirt disappeared for a few years in the middle of the decade, but by 1998, Marc Jacobs and Narcisco Rodriguez, two designers with very different points of view but a similar appreciation of femininity, were cutting strict white shirts and pairing them with knee-length skirts and heels for a modern take on a classic American look (Rodriguez tossed aside the notion of rigorous upkeep when he admitted to *Harper's Bazaar* in 1998 that he liked his white shirts "straight from the dryer, kind of wrinkled.")

In the last few seasons, the embellished blouse—either peasant or Edwardian in flavor—has been the white shirt of choice. Though I appreciate a certain amount of "ethnicity," as fashion refers to clothes not straight out of the Western canon, in my wardrobe, I'm not much for lace, and I don't like clothes that feel like costumes. Consequently, my white shirt collection has remained more or less static in this highly decorative time. But I have no doubt that the pendulum will swing back toward the other extreme, as it has so many times before. Fashion does nothing better than the about-face, especially when confronted with a garment as chic, graphic, and timeless as a white shirt.

The High Heel

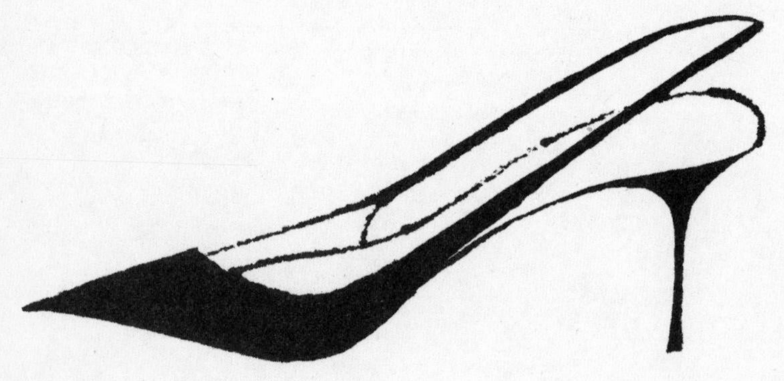

I don't know who invented the high heel but women owe him a lot.

—Marilyn Monroe

WALKING ALONG THE STREET, EVEN ON THE SUNNIEST of days, I often find myself looking down. I'm not searching for stray pennies to enhance my luck or even, prudent New Yorker that I am, avoiding eye contact with potential loons—I'm looking at people's feet. Or, more accurately, their shoes. Some people obsess about food, others about love, still more about money. I am enamoured of shoes.

At this particular moment in history, my penchant is not especially unique—plenty of women, and not a few men, are mad about shoes. Complete strangers of both sexes have run up to me and begged me to tell them where I bought my shoes.

This happens often enough that I can comfortably tell myself that there's nothing unusual about my interest except perhaps its intensity. Not everyone, I understand, is willing to dodge work-bound pedestrians for a block to get a second look at a pair of pumps. (When I find myself doing this I rationalize that it's all in the name of research.) But my curiosity is not motivated by aesthetics alone. I may admire a finely curved instep for its sheer beauty, but the real reason I find shoes fascinating is that they are so revealing. Look at a person's shoes and you can guess her emotional state; her goals and expectations; whether her self-esteem is high or low; and, most significantly, her attitude toward sex. Some types of women's shoes, such as loafers and sneakers, are sexually neutral. Women who habitually wear this type of footwear aren't aggressive about advertising their sex appeal. At the opposite extreme are women who only wear shoes that are overtly feminine, which is to say, impractical, uncomfortable, and fragile. The quintessential example of this type of shoe is undoubtedly the high heel.

If you've ever watched a woman in high heels walk down the street, you know what a powerful pull this type of shoe exerts. The rhythm of the high-heel wearer is both auditory and visual, a mesmerizing combination of staccato tapping and swaying hips. Compared with her flat-footed sisters, a woman in high heels is a siren, watched by men and women alike—though often for different reasons. I was once stopped on West Broadway by a fashionably dressed woman who demanded to know how I walked so fast in such high heels. (The answer is to buy well-balanced shoes. When it comes to your feet, you get what you pay for.) I can only guess that she wanted to take advantage of my expertise for herself.

Much as I like them, I don't advocate wearing high heels everyday. I think that's a vulgar habit, akin to wearing strapless tops to the office. But then, whether a heel is high or not is very often in the eye of the beholder. A friend once insisted on giving me a lift home on the grounds that I couldn't possibly walk so far in my high heels. I was genuinely astonished at her concern, as I'd picked out my modest, two-inch sandals precisely because they were so easy to walk in.

Nevertheless, the high heel, by which I mean one that is three inches or higher, has rarely been as popular as it is right now. This is due in part to the minimalist fashions of the mid to late '90s, a time when style was so pared-down that shoes were one of the few accessories deemed permissible by fashion pundits. With color and detail taboo, women turned to shoes to express their personalities. One result of this trend was the emergence of some extremely fanciful shoe designs, including the very high heel.

Of course, what we put on our feet has always been meaningful. In fairy tales, shoes are often a way to escape from the drudgery of day-to-day existence—think of Jack's forty-league boots or Cinderella's glass slipper. In real life shoes symbolize the values of the society that creates them and makes them popular. The constrictive boots worn by Victorian women, for example, were a product of a repressive, patriarchal culture (as, more dramatically, were the bound feet of Chinese women). The meaning of shoes hasn't changed, but in the past ten years or so the subject matter has taken on a previously unrealized importance. Despite its comparatively low cost, the high heel has replaced the diamond bracelet and the fur coat as a symbol of luxury. Today, a woman wearing a pair of high-end designer heels has arrived, in the same way that a woman wearing an ankle-sweeping mink in 1945 had arrived.

That high heels can be beautiful, sexy, and feminine is undeniable. But the defining characteristic of the high heel is not its appearance but its astonishing lack of practical purpose. It is the most anti-utilitarian shoe ever devised—which is precisely what makes it so enticing. While you can certainly learn to walk or even dance in high heels, you can't do very much else except look good. (A point that was made grimly clear in the wake of the 2001 attack on the World Trade Center, when thousands of women cast aside their heels to run for their lives.) Traditionally, the only people who get away with doing nothing are those who enjoy a privileged social position, that is, the wealthy. To wear a high heel is to suggest that you are above even moderately demanding tasks. In effect, the high heel is the modern equivalent of the corset: blatantly frivolous, designed to accentuate the female form, and an indicator of exalted status. To pursue that metaphor a bit further, it's interesting to note that in his seminal 1899 book, *The Theory of the Leisure Class*, Thorstein Veblen lampooned the corset as an example of conspicuous consumption. Veblen castigated the corset because it was designed to make the woman wearing it unable to perform any sort of physical labor while simultaneously emphasizing her ability to act as a sexual object—much the way high heels do now.

With so much symbolic significance concentrated in one accessory, it's only natural that the high heel's profile be raised so dramatically. For even though the dress code has relaxed somewhat to include brighter hues and the odd flounce, the heel's importance as a fashion statement remains unchallenged, so much so that the names of those who design pricey shoes are becoming widely known even outside the rarefied confines of the fashion world. Exclusive shoemakers have always existed, but it is a testament to the current significance attached to the high heel that names such as Jimmy Choo and Manolo Blahnik are almost as well known as that of Madonna (who famously said that Blahniks are better than sex—and they last longer).

Jimmy Choo is a London-based designer of flower-bedecked stiletto pumps and spike-heel boots that retail in the range of $400 to $1,500. Choo has been a favorite of fashionistas for several years, but in 2001 his appeal reached critical mass. That year, on an episode of *The Sopranos*—not a show customarily associated with high style—one of the characters presented his delighted girlfriend with a trash bag full of stolen stilettos. "Does anybody here love the word Jimmy Choo shoes?" he demands. The writers of the scene, Mitchell Burgess and Robin Green, said they picked a brand-name high heel rather than gold or diamonds because they wanted something that really symbolized loot. That the boyfriend actually named the designer of the shoes indicates how elevated Choo's stock is. Just a few months later Choo's name popped up again, this time in a real-life example of high heel mania. In July of that year, a New York publicist named Lizzie Grubman backed her Mercedes SUV into a crowd of fifteen people outside a nightclub. According to *The New York Observer*, one of the injured, a woman who had suffered broken ribs and was wearing an oxygen mask, paused as she was being loaded into an ambulance to beg her friends "to remove her expensive lace-up Jimmy Choo sandals so they wouldn't be cut off by paramedics." Again, the name of the designer was invoked to emphasize the desirability of the shoes. Is it any surprise to learn that Choo rounded out the year by selling his company to Equinox Luxury Holdings for $21 million?

Despite the rather amazing endorsement of the woman in the oxygen mask, Jimmy Choo isn't the most acclaimed member of his profession. That honor goes to the delightfully named Manolo Blahnik, a man perfectly cast in the role of high-end shoe designer. The Blahnik persona encompasses all the accepted tenets of eccentric genius behavior, including obsessive personal habits (he bathes three times a day) and a fondness for cryptic pronouncements ("I'm simply mad for extremities. I always have been. The rest of the body seems so dull to me."). The latter are issued in a voice that has been described by Michael Specter in *The New Yorker* as combining "the diction of Winston Churchill with the accent of the Gabor sisters." Blahnik's shoes are as piquant and unique as their creator, featherweight marvels of leather, velvet, and brocade that sit on the highest and slenderest of heels. The prices for these sublime examples of the shoemaker's art begin at $500. Despite this seemingly prohibitive figure, Blahnik's sales clout is such that the head buyer for women's shoes at Neiman Marcus told Specter that if the designer asked her to change the name of the store to Neiman Blahnik she wouldn't hesitate to do so for a second.

In the early twenty-first century, Manolo Blahniks set the standard by which all other heels are measured. What sets the master's creations apart from all others of their kind is their sheer sexiness. Put on a pair of Blahniks and you automatically start sashaying like Mae West on the make. On the aptly named *Sex and the City*, Blahnik is mentioned so often that the casual viewer could be forgiven for thinking he's the fifth member of the cast. In circles where sex appeal is at a premium, such as fashion and entertainment, Blahniks are as common as cell phones. When a well-known Hollywood stylist fell off hers and broke her arm, *The New York Times* described the accident as an occupational hazard. In scenarios outside of the Tinseltown/Fashionland axis, a Manolo Blahnik reference is used to indicate a person's level of sophistication. Thus, in a *New York* magazine profile of a young yoga instructor at one of the city's trendiest ashrams, the writer quoted her as saying, "If you don't see God in a pair of Manolo Blahniks, then you haven't looked hard enough or you can't afford them."

Blahniks certainly ratchet up the sex appeal of the high heel, but that appeal was pretty spectacular to begin with, a fact that was recognized as far back as the fifteenth century, when the British Parliament passed a law specifying that any woman who beguiled a man into marrying her "through the use of high-heeled shoes or other devices . . . shall be punished with the penalties of witchcraft."

Why are high heels so bewitching? For one thing, in modern times, they are a uniquely feminine form of footwear. Only women—and men dressing up as women, which always involves an exaggeration of feminine characteristics—wear high-heel shoes. Furthermore, high heels put an almost cartoonlike emphasis on a woman's physical attributes. High heels tilt the pelvis, causing the breasts to jut forward and the buttocks to protrude (as much as 25 percent, according to *Harper's* "Index"). They visually elongate the leg, which in turn draws the eye upward, to the genitals. By tightening the lower leg muscles, high-heel shoes slim the calves and ankles. A high heel makes the foot look smaller by positioning it at an extreme angle, which also exaggerates the arch of the instep. Finally, high heels change a woman's gait considerably. By setting the body on an unstable perch, high heels force the wearer to compensate for her lack of balance by taking tiny steps and swinging her hips to counteract the unsteadiness of her feet. It's a potent combination.

Not that all the pleasure of wearing high heels is in the eye of the beholder. Studies indicate that walking in high heels causes the buttocks to undulate more rapidly than walking in flats; this increases the flow of blood to the genitals, mimicking the physiological changes that take place during sexual arousal.

Psychiatrists have limned the connection between high heels and sex, suggesting that women crave high heels as a kind of palliative for penis envy, a conclusion that's based on the hypothesis that the heel of a shoe resembles the male sexual organ. But are women really filling their closets with faux phalluses? Of course not. A woman in heels is fully aware of her feminine power, as actress Ann Magnuson discovered when *Allure* sent her on an expedition down Hollywood Boulevard in four-inch heels in 1994. She wrote, "My breasts jutted forward, while my back was severely arched. My ass felt bigger than a Buick, and my thighs, or, rather, my flanks, swung back and forth like a couple of sides of beef." Yet, she continues, the teetering heels made her feel "mythically omnipotent . . . I felt a surge of power, knowing I could lay waste to any man I chose to destroy."

To some feminists, high heels are a symbol of patriarchal power. They argue that high heels keep women subordinate because they restrict movement. In his novel about a foot fetishist and the object of his desire, *Footsucker*, Geoff Nicholson describes high heels as "fuck-me shoes" because "the woman is saying if you can catch me you can fuck me, and of course, any damn fool can catch a woman in a pair of shoes with six-inch heels." But in foot fetish pornography, the woman wearing the high heels is usually the dominant participant—the kitten with the whip. Since fetish heels can soar to eleven inches, she may not be able to easily escape her partner, but she wields considerable power of her own, making for an ambiguous scenario. A hint of this extremism is evident even in ordinary high heels, which make rapid movement quite difficult. To some, this in itself is exciting. As the fashion photographer David Bailey once said, "I like high heels—I know it's chauvinistic. It means girls can't run away from me."

Another point of view, currently in vogue, is that the high heel is a symbol of power. Today, wearing high heels is closely linked to professional and social prestige. In the '80s, women showed they had power and status by wearing sneakers on the street, changing into heels only when they reached the office, thereby implying that they were too busy being successful to tolerate impractical footwear. The definition of status has since shifted—it now means being pampered, not taking pride in an overscheduled life. By wearing high heels all day long, you send out the message that you don't need to do anything as taxing as taking the subway (or at the very least, you want it to look that way). Which is why we still use the expression "well-heeled" to refer to the wealthy. The wealthy don't have to rush around, and can therefore wear heels to their hearts' content. Conversely, to be poor is to be "down at heel."

The first high heels were the platform shoes worn by actors in ancient Greece. The higher the status of the character portrayed, the higher the shoe, so that from its inception, towering footwear was synonymous with lofty position.

This same type of shoe became very popular in the fifteenth and sixteenth centuries, particularly in Venice, where it was known as a chopine and associated with courtesans. Chopines were worn only by women, and could reach heights of eighteen inches. Perched on these tapering wooden blocks, fashionable women couldn't walk without assistance and were the subject of ridicule by contemporary satirists. The chopine is even mentioned in Shakespeare, when Hamlet snidely remarks to his mother, "Your ladyship is nearer to heaven than when I saw you last, by the height of your chopine." Given Hamlet's contempt for what he sees as his mother's moral depravity—he suspects her of conspiring to murder his father and then marry his uncle—and the chopine's association with prostitutes, his observation is all the more cutting.

Both sexes wore high heels at the fashion-conscious court of Louis XIV. In fact, they were required to: The high heel, preferably in aristocratic red, was the prerogative of the nobility. But as men's clothes became less elaborate, eschewing pastel silks and elaborate embroideries for businesslike wools and precisely knotted cravats, high heels evolved into a potent symbol of femininity. With their feet back on level ground, men's walks became a stride, while the mincing and swaying associated with elevated heels became the sole province of women. Consequently, the high heel took on immense erotic importance to many men.

Shod in high heels or not, the feet have always been linked to sex. In ancient Greece, goddesses were depicted as having the second toe longer than the first, an attribute that hinted at their powerful—that is, masculine—sexuality. The toes, especially the big toe, symbolize the phallus, while the cleft between the toes symbolize the vulva (an association that makes the whole issue of toe cleavage even more disconcerting). The entire foot can be interpreted in sexual terms: It has been described as a quasi penis, to be slipped into the feminine embrace of the shoe. In *Footsucker*, Nicholson describes a foot that is "as taut and veined as an engorged penis."

The foot scholar William Rossi suggests that the association of the human foot with sex is a result of its unique structure. In his oddly engaging book *The Sex Life of the Foot and Shoe*, he argues that the shape of our feet allows us to stand upright, and, therefore, to engage in frontal copulation. Humans are the only species to have intercourse face to face, and since this ability stems directly from our feet, it's no wonder that we're so sexually preoccupied with them. Indeed, foot worship is the most common sexual fetish. Rossi quotes Havelock Ellis, who wrote, "Of all the forms of erotic symbolism, the most frequent is that which idealizes the foot and shoe . . . It would seem that even for the normal lover, the foot is one of the most attractive parts of the body."

With its curvy arch, instep, and ankles, the foot certainly provides visual stimulus. But its connection to sex is more deeply ingrained, as Dr. Valerie Steele explains in her book *Shoes: A Lexicon of Style.* In the 1940s, she writes, Dr. Wilder Penfield, a well-known neurosurgeon, mapped out the areas of the brain that correspond to various parts of the body. By stimulating the area of the brain that related to the arm, for example, Penfield observed a reaction in that part of the body. His research showed that, for the most part, the map on the surface of the brain followed the shape of the body. But the area that relates to sensation in the genitals is not, as would be expected, between the thighs, but next to the feet. Steele goes on to quote Dr. V. S. Ramachandran, who expanded on Penfield's research in *Phantoms in the Brain: Probing the Mysteries of the Human Mind.* Ramachandran relates that amputees who have lost their legs report feeling sensations in their phantom feet during sex—one man even claimed that he felt an orgasm in his missing foot. These associations are obviously deep-seated.

No culture went further in eroticizing the foot than China, where foot binding was considered not only beautiful, but sexually arousing; a man would kiss and fondle his lover's stunted foot, and even insert his penis into the fleshy crevice created by the artificially rounded arch. In the West, a small foot was considered a prerequisite for physical attraction. In seventeenth- and eighteenth-century France and England, it was judged a mark of nobility, and portrait sitters were routinely painted with abbreviated, idealized feet. In the middle of the nineteenth century, when fashionable women strove to look as fragile and childlike as possible, the tiny foot was also much desired, and fashionable coquettes forced their feet into shoes that were several sizes too small. An unfortunate side effect of this practice can be seen in the fashion plates of the time, which show ankles bulging above snugly buttoned booties.

Though most women are now too tall to have child-sized feet, the preference for small feet hasn't gone away. In its July 2000 issue *Vogue* asserted—in a story illustrated with a diamond-encrusted Jimmy Choo stiletto sandal modeled on a perfectly tanned leg—that the ideal feet are "light-boned . . . sized 7 or 8. (These are the dimensions best suited to the structure of a Manolo Blahnik stiletto. Feet any bigger are considered too gargantuan to be truly pretty.)"

The ultimate small-foot story is Cinderella, in which a Lilliputian extremity results in marriage to a prince. In the original version, by Charles Perrault, the ugly stepsisters are so determined to fit into Cinderella's miniscule slipper that they cut off their toes and heels in the attempt—the blood seeping through the sole of the shoe gives them away as clodhopper imposters. In the 1960s, fashion photographer William Klein satirized this impulse to downplay the size of the foot in the name of beauty in his film *Qui êtes-vous, Polly Magoo?* Klein has a character theorize that the Cinderella story is about "the value of tiny feet and beautiful clothes." He concludes by announcing, "So there you are: fetishism, mutilation, pain. Fashion in a nutshell!"

It was only after World War I that women's shoes came into more or less constant view. Prior to the 1920s, women's shoes didn't change very much from year to year. The fabulous collection of Rita Lydig, a famed American beauty of the Gilded Age, while spectacular, has a disappointing uniformity. Her delicate shoes, designed by the legendary shoemaker Yatourney, all have two-and-a-half-inch Louis Quinze heels, softly pointed toes, and high vamps. It wasn't that Lydig didn't appreciate stylish shoes—she once remarked that a shoe without sex appeal was like a tree without leaves, barren—but that in her time, fashion simply wasn't focused on the feet. In our shoe-crazed era, this may be hard to fathom. How could a fashionable woman not love shoes, we marvel. Easy—she had lots of other accessories, all highly visible, to fuss over. Hidden beneath layers of skirt and petticoat, shoes were selected for quality, not style.

But with the lifting of hemlines in the 1920s, shoes and hosiery took on new importance. Sheer, flesh-colored stockings that imitated nudity became popular, and heels grew higher, to better showcase the newly exposed ankle. Color, too, became an important feature of shoes. Once restricted to practical shades of brown and black, footwear in all colors of the rainbow was now available. By the 1930s, women routinely wore heels. Even war rationing couldn't stop this trend. When leather and wood became scarce, shoemakers turned out cork-soled wedgies, a style that is even now associated with the war years.

The ultimate high heel, the stiletto, was invented in the early 1950s, when an Italian manufacturer developed a heel with a metal core, an innovation that allowed for the skinniest heels ever devised. Towering yet delicate looking, the stiletto is what most people have in mind when they think of high heels. It's constrictive, difficult to walk in, and prone to snap under pressure—inconveniences that do nothing to deter women from wearing it. When it first appeared, the stiletto was criticized by doctors for causing back problems and was banned from some public buildings because of the damage it inflicted on floors, but its popularity was immediate. The sinuous walk it prompted was the ideal accompaniment to the ultrafeminine clothes of the era; along with wasp waists and pushed-up bosoms, the stiletto is femininity incarnate. When it's not in vogue—as it wasn't in the early '70s and the mid-'80s—the stiletto is the tackiest shoe imaginable, on par with peroxided hair and sequined sweaters. But when the stiletto is hot, nothing can touch it.

The stiletto made a significant comeback in the fall of 1997, when Tom Ford designed a pointy, metal-tipped patent leather style for Gucci. Gucci's ad campaign that season resembled surveillance footage, with grainy, washed-out images that hinted at voyeurism, and gave viewers the impression that they were witnessing something they shouldn't. The shoe caused a frenzy, and waiting lists for it stretched on for pages. After years of chunky-heeled shoes, introduced by Prada and copied by everyone else, the novelty of the stiletto made it the shoe of the season. For fall 2002, Tom Ford raised the stiletto to fresh heights, sending his models out in five-inch heels. Compounded by a shag carpet runway, this led to some awkward moments. One unfortunate model fell three times, prompting an observer to announce dramatically that her career was over.

What made Gucci's 1997 stiletto particularly provocative was its bladelike metal heel, which closely resembled the knife for which the shoe is named. Like the stiletto shoe, the stiletto knife is associated with sexual intensity—specifically, hot-blooded crimes of passion. In vintage crime novels, it's the vengeful lover, male or female, who wields this weapon. If the stiletto user is a man, you can be sure he will be described as a Latin or an Italian—who were then felt to be more feminine and unstable than red-blooded Americans or Brits.

The similarity between the shoe and the blade was made deadly clear in the film *Single White Female.* In the movie, Jennifer Jason Leigh, playing a mousy introvert, covets her roommate, fashion-industry-success-story Bridget Fonda's life and boyfriend. Leigh imitates Fonda's mannerisms and taste, even buying black stiletto pumps identical to a pair Fonda owns. At several points in the narrative, the camera lingers on the shoes, fetishising their dark sexiness. Finally, wearing the pumps, Leigh tricks and seduces Fonda's boyfriend. When he turns on her, she stabs him to death with the heel of her shoe. Like the female scorpion, Leigh's character is the deadlier of the species.

Perhaps seeking to avoid a real-life version of this situation, in the fall of 2001 Manolo Blahnik canceled plans for a potentially lethal stiletto. The shoe in question had a three-and-a-half-inch titanium heel the diameter of a narrow knitting needle. "The heel was easy to walk on and steady but would cut through carpet. If the wearer stood on someone's foot, it would go straight through," a spokesman for Blahnik explained. There was also a chance the shoes could be mistaken for weapons by airport X-ray machines, the final straw in Blahnik's decision to yank the shoe from the market. Deterred but undaunted, he planned to redesign the shoe with a safer heel.

Though imagining a shoe as a murder weapon may seem like a stretch, a woman in a very high, thin heel does look as though she has a deadly object attached to her foot. As Ann Magnuson memorably described in *Allure*, walking around in a pair of heels is a power trip. It's the feminine equivalent of packing heat. In the right heels, a woman feels invincible.

James Herlihy ascribed a similar effect to Joe Buck's shoes in his novel *Midnight Cowboy*, which was later made into an Oscar-winning film starring Jon Voigt. Though the passage refers to a pair of cowboy boots, it could just as easily be describing a pair of four-inch heels. (Cowboy boots are one of the only remaining acceptable high-heel shoe styles for men—the rationale is that the heel helps to keep the foot firmly in the stirrup. Psychologically, the heel on cowboy boots works because cowboys are presumably so masculine that they can get away with it.) After purchasing the boots, Buck, a small town hick, suddenly feels the sexual frisson that comes with stepping into the right shoes: "Something snapped in the whole bottom half of him: A kind of power he never even knew was there had been released in his pelvis and he was able to feel the world through it. Brand-new muscles came into play in his buttocks and in his legs, and he was aware of a totally new attitude toward the sidewalk. The world was down there, and he was up here, on top of it, and the space between him and it was now commanded by a beautiful strange animal, himself, Joe Buck. He was strong. He was exultant. He was ready."

I've experienced this kind of metamorphosis myself. Several years ago, I was in a shoe store trying to decide whether to buy a pair of extravagant black calfskin slingbacks with three-and-a-half-inch heels. It was late November, just past dusk on a dreary day, and I was the only customer in the shop. They were elegant, almost severely so, and by far the most grown-up pair of shoes I'd ever contemplated purchasing. They had a thin heel, a tapered toe, and a voluptuously shaped instep. The slingback hugged the back of my ankle, emphasizing the tautness of the Achilles tendon and the slender curve of the calf. Standing there in them, I felt feminine but powerful—these were definitely a woman's shoes, not a girl's. My cast-off boots, sprawled on the floor next to the mirror, seemed completely inadequate in comparison. For several long minutes, the salesman and I stared at my sublimely shod feet in meditative silence. Finally, he spoke. "Those are serious shoes," he said. I nodded, my mind made up. "I'll take them."

I haven't regretted my decision for a minute.

Pearls

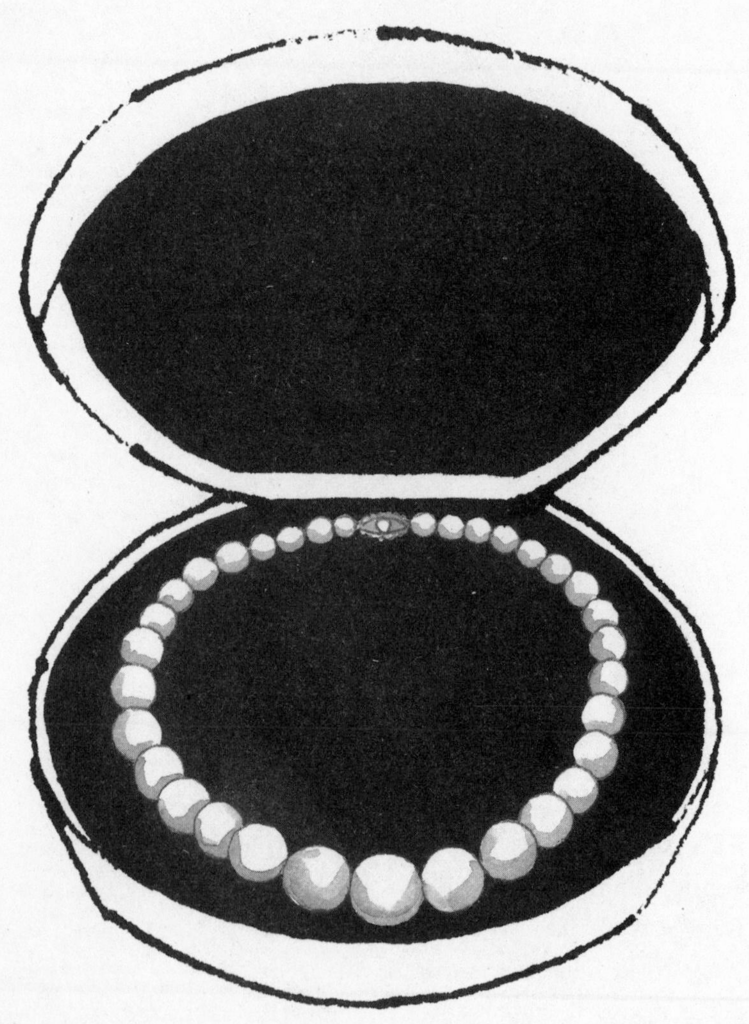

Pearls give a gloss, a certain refinement, even if you're just a trashy girl.

—Manolo Blahnik

IN 1923, TO WIN OVER HER FIANCÉ REGGIE VANDERBILT'S mother, Gloria Morgan—who would later give birth to designer jeans doyenne Gloria Vanderbilt—underwent a medical examination to certify her virginity. To the delight of the Vanderbilt matriarch, Gloria passed the test, and she and Reggie were invited to lunch at the Ambassador Hotel in New York. During the course of the meal, Mrs. Vanderbilt asked if Gloria had "received her pearls yet." When Reggie confessed that he couldn't afford the kind of pearls Gloria should have, Mrs. Vanderbilt summoned a waiter and asked for a pair of scissors. She then took off the hefty rope of pearls that looped twice around her neck and hung to her waist, cut off a third—about $70,000 worth—and handed the freed strand to her future daughter-in-law. "There you are, Gloria," she said. "All the Vanderbilt women have pearls."

The Vanderbilt women were famous for their pearls. Gertrude Vanderbilt Whitney, Gloria's sister-in-law and the founder of the Whitney Museum of American Art, had a necklace that was estimated to be worth $600,000. It was a wedding present from one of her husband's uncles, who was a member of the Payne family. Gertrude's cousin Consuelo Vanderbilt, who in 1895 was pushed into marrying the ninth Duke of Marlborough—her mother thought it would be nice to have a title in the family—had a five-hundred-pearl necklace that once belonged to Empress Eugenie of France, another that had been worn by Catherine the Great, and a lengthy pearl *sautoir* that doubled as a belt. And that was just what she got from her family as compensation for marrying the unappealing Duke (they also posted guards outside her bedroom door the night before the wedding, to prevent her escape). Consuelo later acquired a magnificent but apparently very uncomfortable nineteen-strand pearl collar that reached from the base of her throat to her chin. She was so associated with her pearls that when John Singer Sargent painted her without them, her friends were shocked. In her memoir, *The Glitter and the Gold*, Consuelo writes that one of her sisters-in-law, scandalized by her naked throat, took her aside and told her that she should never appear in public without them.

Even today, we associate pearls with ladies. Diamonds may be a girl's best friend, but a string of pearls is the badge of a lady. Diamonds, with their hard-edged glitter, suggest a reward for services well rendered. Pearls, on the other hand, are subtle. Their unmistakable gleam is discreet, you can wear them to breakfast, it takes a pro to tell the real from the fake, and they carry an unmistakable whiff of old money, even if you bought them yourself with your first paycheck. According to the fashion designer Donald Brooks, quoted in *People and Pearls*, Ki Hackney and Diana Edkins's book about the luminous orbs and the women who love them, "You can turn an absolute whore into a lady by just putting pearls around her neck." That's a bit of a stretch, but pearls are certainly a tried-and-true Hollywood prop—any time a character is supposed to come across as proper and traditional, you can be sure she'll have a string of pearls fastened about her neck. As Lyn Williams, a pearl wearer and "highly respected civic leader based in New York City and Sag Harbor" consulted by Hackney and Edkins says, "When you see someone wearing pearls, you assume they share a certain set of traditional values; that they are solid and reliable."

Like many ladies, pearls appear fragile but are really quite tough—provided they are properly cared for. They should be the last thing you put on before you leave the house and the first thing you take off when you return. Pearls react adversely to perfume, oil, chlorine, hairspray, and perspiration, so they should be wiped with a soft cloth after every outing. Yet their round shape makes them incredibly resilient. One method merchants used to determine real pearls from imitations was to stomp on them. A fake would crumble, while a genuine pearl would roll away unscathed.

The pearl's faultless reputation stems from the fact that it is naturally perfect. Unlike diamonds or emeralds or sapphires, pearls don't need any special polishing or finishing to look stunning; that's just the way they are. This has made them a powerful symbol of purity and innocence, an association that is underscored by their watery origins. We associate water with renewal, and, consequently, pearls are often given to a woman when she's reached some sort of milestone: a sixteenth birthday, graduation, marriage, the birth of a child. In *The First Wives Club*, Diane Keaton, Bette Midler, and Goldie Hawn wear matching pearl necklaces that they received as college graduates; that they're still wearing them twenty-five years later is a reminder of their strong ties and shared values. Pearls were as common in engagement rings in the nineteenth century as diamonds are today, and the pearl is the gemstone for June, still the most popular month for weddings.

I have a pearl ring that belonged to my great-grandmother, who died when she was only thirty-two; my grandmother gave it to me when I got engaged. I also have a pearl pendant my sister gave me when I was her maid of honor. My string of pearls were a high school graduation gift from my mother. They're a twenty-four-inch strand of seven-millimeter Akoyas, a length optimistically known as matinee (I've never actually worn them to a matinee). Pearl necklaces are classified according to their lengths, and the names tend to be rather romantic. A princess strand, for example, is between seventeen and nineteen inches long, while an opera one ranges from twenty-eight to thirty-four inches in length. The most extravagant of all is the *sautoir* which is at least forty-five inches long and often has hidden clasps that allow you to divide it into multiple strands or bracelets. Alternately, you can wear it in one glorious fall, as Louise Brooks did in a famous photograph taken in the 1920s. In the photo, Brooks stands in profile, holding the necklace around her neck in an outstretched hand. Her dress, the wall behind her, and her smooth cap of hair are all black, so that the pearls shine like stars against the night sky.

I'm not much of a jewelry wearer, so my pearls rarely leave their blue velvet box. Nevertheless, I like knowing they're there—they are part of what links me to the other women in my family. This is not an uncommon sentiment. In researching this chapter, I've come across dozens of stories of pearls being handed down from mother to daughter to granddaughter—some spectacular, like the Vanderbilt tale, others more ordinary but no less meaningful. Pearls are a singularly graceful legacy, not just a possession but an emblem of femininity. (Because they're so widely recognized as such, pearls are the perfect tool for turning concepts like gentility on their heads: Tim Curry, playing the sex-mad transvestite Dr. Frankenfurter in *The Rocky Horror Picture Show*, wore a neat pearl choker.)

Whenever I do have occasion to wear my pearls, people are invariably drawn to comment on them. A dapper elderly man once approached me at a wedding to tell me that I reminded him of his mother as a young woman. He related that she had a similar strand, and wore them all the time. There is something about pearls—their air of cleanliness, their association with femininity, their purity of color and form—that is very inviting. Pearls are high-status enough to be aspirational, yet familiar enough to inspire warmth.

I once had a job that involved calling up pharmacies and department stores to see if they would be interested in carrying a moisturizer that contained crushed pearls. Though no one I spoke to had ever heard of such a thing, everyone was captivated by the idea. In retrospect, I understand their reaction. Pearls made the cream sound so . . . promising. Who wouldn't want pearly skin? Chinese women stir crushed pearl into their tea in the hopes of attaining just such a complexion. If the magic ingredient in the cream had been diamonds I don't think the interest would have been the same. Diamonds are far too knowing. Pearls, on the other hand, exert a high-minded and wistful pull on the imagination. You want to believe that they have magical properties.

For example, in Jean Giraudoux's 1947 play *The Madwoman of Chaillot*, a fable about a dotty countess who saves Paris from an unscrupulous businessman, a trio of elderly ladies reminisce about their youthful exploits. When the countess challenges one about the authenticity of her boasts, she cries, "How dare you question my memories? What if I said your pearls were false?" The countess assures her that the pearls were indeed once fakes, but, "Everyone knows that when you wear pearls, little by little they become real." As the action unfolds, and we see that those who appear mad are revealed to be quite sane, and vice versa, the countess's remark becomes less obscure. In this scheme of things, it makes perfect sense that fake pearls could become real. Yet if Giraudoux had chosen rubies or emeralds as the countess's signature jewel, her remark would have struck a false note. In the realm of make-believe, some things are plausible and others just don't ring true. Pearls are mysterious enough to be magical; hard-edged stones are far too earthbound.

Indeed, pearls were once thought to have supernatural origins. The Romans, who were crazy about pearls, believed that they originated with the birth of Venus. According to myth, as she emerged from the sea, the drops of water that fell from her body were transformed into pearls. Ironically, there's nothing mystical or dreamy about the way pearls are made. To be blunt, they're a by-product of the bodily functions of bivalves. Pearls are formed in reaction to particles that get trapped in the shells of oysters and other mollusks and irritate their soft flesh. The irritant is rarely the poetic sounding grain of sand—it's far more likely to be a miniscule crab or some other parasite. To neutralize the irritant, the oyster secretes a dark substance called conchiolin. This envelops the intrusive element in a smooth coating and stimulates the production of nacre, a milky liquid that hardens to form the pearl. The oyster covers the irritant in layer after layer of nacre; if you were to cut a pearl in half, you would see rings similar to the ones found in trees. Each ring is a coating of nacre. The pearl's luster comes from the way light is refracted when it travels through these layers. The more layers a pearl has, the more it glows. Widely spaced layers of nacre, a side-effect of warm water, refract the light more than do tightly packed ones, which is why South Sea pearls are renowned for their opalescent splendor.

Though pearls are commonly thought of as white, they can be any one of a rainbow of colors, including red, pink, yellow, and black. The larger a pearl grows, the more likely it is to be baroque, or irregularly shaped rather than spherical. The largest pearl ever found, the Pearl of Allah, measures 9 inches across and weighs in at 14 pounds. It resembles a hard, glossy brain. Finding two baroque pearls that match is extremely unlikely, which is why perfectly paired pear-shaped pearl earrings are especially prized.

When the production of nacre happens spontaneously, the result is a natural pearl. Natural pearls are so rare that only approximately one in ten thousand oysters will yield one good enough to use in jewelry. A pearl diver could spend a lifetime searching for enough matching pearls to assemble a necklace and fail. This scarcity made pearls especially prized and contributed to their great value. Today, only about 0.5 percent of all pearls sold are natural. These fabulously expensive specimens are usually snapped up by collectors before ever reaching the open market.

The other 99.5 percent of pearls sold are cultured. The culturing process—by which an irritant is deliberately inserted into the oyster to prompt the production of nacre—was understood as much as three thousand years ago by the Chinese. Chinese monks made mother-of-pearl figurines of the Buddha by placing small lead figures of the Enlightened One into oyster shells. But pearl culturing was haphazard and unpredictable until the process was refined by Kokichi Mikimoto in Japan in the 1890s. The technique perfected by Mikimoto continues to be used today. Basically, a tiny ball of mussel shell and a piece of tissue from another mollusk are implanted into an oyster. This tissue, called the mantle, is what will produce the nacre. Once these two elements are inserted into the oyster, the creature is placed in a cage and returned to the ocean. After two to three years—or as little as eight months for the lower quality variety—the pearls are harvested.

Only a trained eye can tell the difference between a pearl produced by this method and a naturally occurring one, but Mikimoto's wares were rejected as fakes when he first tried to sell them. However, by the 1920s natural pearls were so rare that it took a jeweler ten years to assemble sixty-three matching natural pearls for a necklace John D. Rockefeller gave his wife in 1929. This depleted world stock, combined with Mikimoto's determined campaign to make cultured pearls acceptable, eventually swayed public opinion. By the 1930s cultured pearls were accepted as real pearls, with Mikimoto cornering the market. Even today, when Australia, Taiwan, Myanmar, and China are also large producers of pearls, Japanese technicians dominate the pearl industry.

Imitation pearls date back to ancient times. The techniques for making them varied but the one that is still used originated in Paris in the eighteenth century. It involves mixing iridescent fish scales—today, it's more likely to be a synthetic equivalent—with lacquer to make a liquid called *essence d'orient*. Glass beads are then dipped repeatedly into this mixture, which produces a luster comparable to that of true pearls. The punishments for trying to pass off fake pearls as authentic were inevitably harsh. In medieval Venice, for example, where pearl mania was especially pronounced, a merchant who tried to swindle a customer in this way faced the loss of a hand and a ten-year exile.

This stiff penalty indicates how highly prized real pearls were. Cleopatra once placed a wager with her lover, Marc Antony, that involved a perfect pearl. She bet him that she could serve him the most expensive meal ever made. As dinner was served, Cleopatra removed one of her prized pearl earrings and dissolved it in a glass of wine (she must have dispatched a handy servant to grind it down first because wine will not dissolve a pearl). She downed the concoction, then offered Marc Antony the other earring so he could do the same. Acknowledging defeat, he declined. According to Pliny the Elder, Cleopatra's pearl cocktail was worth the equivalent of eighty thousand Roman pounds of gold.

Others imbibe pearls not for showmanship but for good health. Mikimoto, for one, had two pulverized pearls in a glass of vinegar every morning for breakfast from the time he was twenty until his death at the age of ninety-six. Whether the pearls contributed to his longevity or not is unclear, though they certainly don't seem to have done him any harm. Pearls are composed mainly of calcium carbonate, the same ingredient used in antacids, so if nothing else, Mikimoto's daily treat kept indigestion at bay.

Marc Antony no doubt knew the value of the pearl Cleopatra had sacrificed, as pearls were very popular with the Romans. Julius Caesar even passed sumptuary laws preventing anyone below the rank of patrician from wearing real ones. This was intended to keep pearls on the necks and ears of the aristocracy, but by the first century C.E., they were the most popular jewel in the far-flung Roman Empire.

Even the early Christians, who led rather less glamorous lives than the Caesars, recognized the value of pearls. Expressions such as "pearls of wisdom" and "a pearl among women" originate in the Bible, which makes frequent use of the pearl as a metaphor. In the Sermon on the Mount, Christ equates the pearl with wisdom when he says, "The Kingdom of Heaven is like a merchant searching for beautiful pearls, who finding one at great cost, sells all his possessions to buy it." To the true believer, the wisdom that the pearl symbolizes is more valuable than any worldly belongings, because it will result in his entry into paradise.

Perhaps Ferdinand and Isabella, the pious Spanish monarchs who financed Christopher Columbus's voyages, had such images in mind when they put pearls on the top of the list of goods they expected Columbus to bring back from his wanderings. But it's more likely that greed played the dominant role in their orders. Like their peers across Europe, Ferdinand and Isabella were mad about pearls. They knew that whoever discovered a fresh source for the rare gems would make a fortune, for even then, demand far exceeded supply. It wasn't until his third trip, in 1498, that Columbus discovered rich pearl beds off the coast of what is now Venezuela. His find set off a pearl frenzy that lasted for 150 years, a period in which more pearls entered circulation than at any time before or since. In standard conquering-invader style, the rush lasted until the Venezuelan pearl beds were completely depleted.

Royal portraits of the sixteenth century offer ample evidence of the era's love of pearls: Both men and women are covered in them. The ultimate royal pearl lover was undoubtedly Elizabeth I of England, whose weakness for them is often alluded to in contemporary accounts; she once demanded that a noblewoman hand over her pearl-embroidered black velvet dress. But even Elizabeth could never afford as many pearls as she craved, so she employed a crew of seamstresses who did nothing but transfer pearls from one sumptuous dress to another (she also reputedly rounded out her collection with fakes). Pearls were her personal emblem—a shrewd choice for the self-proclaimed Virgin Queen. Elizabeth never married, claiming that England was her beloved. In return, her subjects adored her. Elizabeth's love of pearls grew in proportion to her power. A portrait of her at the age of thirteen shows a young girl with a modest allowance of pearls. By the time of the *Armada Portrait,* painted in 1588 to commemorate the British naval victory over the Spanish, Elizabeth wears, in addition to the pearls covering her clothes and woven into her hair, eight ropes of pearls that reach to her waist. She looks every inch the triumphant monarch. Clearly, Elizabeth understood the value of spectacle as a necessary tool of government.

As pearls flooded the European market, officials strove in vain to maintain their exclusivity. In Venice, the city government passed a law that specified that only upper-class women in the first fifteen years of marriage could wear them. When that didn't work, they resorted to more draconian measures, and demanded that all the ladies of Venice, other than the dogeressa, her daughters, and her daughters-in-law, hand over their pearls. Apparently, most women turned in their imitation pearls and kept the real thing for themselves, despite the harsh penalty for trying to pass off fake pearls as authentic.

The middle-class acquisition of pearls was especially

marked in the Netherlands, which had a flourishing merchant class. Eager to demonstrate their wealth, many of these prosperous citizens sat for portraits or commissioned portraits of their wives and daughters. What is probably the most famous pearl in art history was painted at this time (1669) in Jan Vermeer's *Girl with a Pearl Earring*. Her pearl is a luminous drop that glows creamily against the dark brush strokes of Vermeer's canvas. Other women posed with their pearl necklaces, as the *Regentesses of the Orphanage in Amsterdam* did for Adriaen Becker in 1683. Three of the four ringleted, soberly dressed women wear single-strand chokers; the fourth wears a double-strand one. All wear pearl bracelets, as well. They look as solid and respectable as a gathering of the Junior League, circa 1955.

The simple necklaces worn by the four women were typical of the new way of wearing pearls that arose in the second half of the seventeenth century. Rather than piling them on by the bushel, fashionable women wore a single, unornamented strand, a style that was probably due to the dwindling supply of pearls. By the time Marie-Antoinette posed for Élisabeth Vigée-Lebrun wearing a single strand of perfectly matched pearls in 1785, the once-abundant Venezuelan pearl beds were a distant memory. Though a pearl necklace was still a status symbol, its fabulousness had been supplanted by the beauty of diamonds, which, thanks to the development of more sophisticated faceting techniques, sparkled more brilliantly than ever before.

Then in the nineteenth century fresh pearl sources were discovered in Australia and Tahiti, and pearls bounced back into the public eye. It was in this period, when ideas about decorum and appropriate behavior were especially strict, that pearls became linked with refinement, good taste, and other ladylike qualities. White pearls, with their virginal associations, were the only jewelry an unmarried woman could wear, and black pearls were considered one of the few ornaments suitable for a widow—the other was jet, which was derived from coal and was also black—after she'd completed her jewelry-free first year of mourning. Mourning customs have all but disappeared, but ideas about pearls and innocence have proven harder to dispel—even today, a sixteen-year-old girl in a pearl choker wouldn't cause any comment; the same girl wearing a similar design in diamonds would raise eyebrows.

The Gilded Age, which began in the 1870s and lasted until World War I, was a spectacular period for pearls. In this pre-income-tax golden age, families such as the Vanderbilts and the Rockefellers accumulated enormous fortunes. They used their wives and daughters to advertise their great wealth by covering them with jewels and outrageously expensive gowns. In an era that inspired the term conspicuous consumption, more was always better than less. A 1900 photograph of the wife of the financier Jay Gould, a former actress named Edith Kingdon, shows her wearing a low-cut, tightly corseted white satin gown trimmed with pearls. Around her neck is a ten-strand collar and three ropes of pearls that were estimated to have cost $500,000. But Mrs. Gould had nothing on Mrs. Mortimer Plant, who in 1916 persuaded her husband to trade their townhouse at the corner of Fifty-second Street and Fifth Avenue for a $1.2 million strand of perfectly matched natural pearls from Cartier. Cartier came out ahead on this deal: The beaux arts mansion still houses the company's New York headquarters. After Mrs. Plant's death in 1957, the necklace was sold at auction. It fetched less than a quarter of a million dollars, as by that time the culturing process had made matched pearls much more common.

One of the pastimes of the rich in the Gilded Age was horse racing. Fashionable men and women flocked to tracks such as Longchamps, in France. It was here that Coco Chanel began her rise to social prominence—and very likely where she saw her first pearls. At the time, she was a poor, convent-bred orphan, just beginning her climb as the second mistress of a wealthy playboy. He wasn't particularly lavish with his gifts, so Chanel didn't actually own any pricey jewels yet herself. But she had her sights set on bigger things. Since she scorned the overly fussy styles of the day, she may already have had ideas about how she would wear pearls if she had a chance. Once Chanel did amass her collection, pearls never looked the same again. As Christian Dior put it, "With a black pullover and 10 rows of pearls she revolutionized fashion."

The pullover and pearls Dior refers to were famously photographed in the 1920s while Chanel holidayed in the south of France. The photo is the antithesis of the image of the lush Mrs. Gould. While Mrs. Gould is porcelain pale and padded with flesh, Chanel is deeply tanned and lean as a boy. The former wears a formal white satin gown, cinched in to show off a tiny waist and substantial breasts. The latter wears trousers and perches on the shoulder of a handsome young man. Moreover, Chanel's pearls are an indiscriminate mix of priceless and fake. Every woman, Chanel said, should have ropes and ropes of pearls; if they were fake, well then, so what? It was the effect that mattered. Chanel wore a mix of real and imitation pearls with her little black dresses, with slacks, with the tiered gypsy skirts she designed in the '30s and the strict suits she created in the '50s. The effect was casual, chic, and very modern. As with her other fashion innovations, Chanel was iconoclastic. She transformed the popular association of pearls with privilege and wealth into that of an affordable delight for all women.

Over the course of the next thirty years, pearls, true and false, were worn by women of every income bracket and taste. Eleanor Roosevelt wore pearls, as did Mamie Eisenhower. Debutantes such as Brenda Frazier wore them, and so did actresses such as Joan Crawford. Any list of the mid-twentieth century's most stylish women includes habitual pearl wearers: the Duchess of Windsor, Babe Paley, C. Z. Guest, Grace Kelly, Jacqueline Kennedy, Audrey Hepburn—all relied on their pearls. In 1947, Irving Penn photographed the twelve most popular models of the previous decade. Seven of this formidably elegant group wore pearls. Even the picky Geneviève Antoine-Dariaux, author of *Elegance,* gave pearls a thumbs-up: "The ideal necklace, the most universally becoming piece of jewelry ever created, and an indispensable accessory in every woman's wardrobe, is a string of pearls," she uncharacteristically gushed.

But while Antoine-Dariaux was writing her book, the rules and customs that had made pearls so essential were losing their hold. By the mid-1960s, a girl was as likely to wear lovebeads as she was to wear pearls. The 1960s and 1970s were not a popular time to be a lady. Women, even those who owned pearls, talked about being women rather than ladies. In an ad for her extremely popular wrap-dress of the early '70s, for example, Diane von Furstenberg posed in one of her creations and a sizable strand of pearls. "Feel like a woman, wear a dress," proclaimed the accompanying copy.

It wasn't until the 1980s that pearls regained some of their lost appeal, when the jaw-breaker-sized South Sea variety became a symbol of yuppie success. Julia Reid, writing in *Vogue*, called these "big girl pearls," nothing like the demure 0.2-inch variety worn by white-gloved debutantes in the 1950s. South Sea pearls drew attention to themselves in a way that more discreet pearls never could; their value, for one thing, was unmistakable. In her *Vogue* article, Reed describes lusting after a $95,000 strand. First Lady Barbara Bush made this type of pearl her signature—though hers were expensive fakes made by Kenneth Jay Lane. South Sea pearls are still a status symbol among socialites, even young ones such as Marie-Chantal Miller, who has been photographed in these pricey jewels by celebrity portraitist David Seidner. She also wears pastel suits and in general projects a rather matronly air—not exactly the way most young women wish to appear.

But in the past few years pearls have been seen on quite fashionable and youthful figures. Pearls were one of the few pieces of jewelry ever seen on the influential Carolyn Bessette Kennedy, a beacon of the minimalist style of the mid-'90s. Well-groomed, twentysomething actresses such as Reese Witherspoon make red-carpet appearances in pearls. Diane von Furstenberg's wrap dresses, which have been adopted by a new generation, are being advertised with the original "feel like a woman" ads—complete with the pearl necklace. And *Lucky*, a magazine that catalogs fashion's seasonal must-haves for a young, female readership, has run several stories about pearls. In February 2001, *Lucky* featured a pearl-buying guide, which discussed luster, surface, and color. A year later, the magazine gave pearl necklaces to four young fashionistas and photographed the way they wove them into their personal style, which included denim corsets and tweed caps. "The ladies who lunch wear them with their pale suits, but matched with more modern pieces, pearls prove to be a totally unstuffy accessory," the editors reported. In 2002, Rimmel, a British cosmetics line, unveiled a print campaign featuring Kate Moss wearing a chestful of pearls that, whether by chance or by design, bear a remarkable resemblance to those worn by Chanel in her groundbreaking 1920s photo. The ad ran in such cutting-edge publications as *Dazed and Confused*, a magazine whose name suggests its readers indulge in activities that would bring a blush to the cheek of a traditional lady. And in 2001, the Chanel jewelry collection included a tough-looking, knuckle-duster pearl ring. All of this indicates that pearls are as popular as ever.

However, as we ease into the twenty-first century, being a lady has taken on a rather different meaning. Etiquette books such as *How to Be a Lady, The Fabulous Girl's Guide to Decorum*, and *Things You Need to Be Told* (the last by a duo calling themselves the Etiquette Girls) are filled with advice on behaving like one. According to these books, any woman aspiring to that title has to know how to negotiate a raise, handle a boyfriend's request to watch porn, and make a killer martini. Not easy tasks. If you're going to attempt them, there's something to be said for having a good string of pearls around your neck.

The Trench Coat

Put on a trench, you're suddenly Audrey Hepburn walking along the Seine—even if you've got red hair and you're five-one.

—Michael Kors

EVERYONE HAS AN IMAGE IN MIND WHEN THEY PULL out their trench coat—figuratively speaking, it's a loaded garment. You might be thinking of Audrey Hepburn in *Breakfast at Tiffany's* or Catherine Deneuve in *The Umbrellas of Cherbourg* or Jane Fonda in *Klute,* all of whom had a way with a trench. My trench coat icon is Jean Shrimpton, the 1960s model who was the face of swinging London. Specifically, Jean Shrimpton on Tower Bridge, as photographed by David Bailey for British *Vogue* in 1962. The duo would go on to become famous as the creators of many of the decade's indelible images, but this early, black-and-white photo has a much scruffier appeal than those later shots. Shrimpton was only eighteen at the time, and she has a coltish, slightly splay-legged awkwardness that makes her seem far more approachable than the coolly perfect, untouchable creature of the later sessions. In the photo Shrimpton appears startled, as though she'd looked up and unexpectedly come face to face with Bailey and his camera. Her hands, deep in her pockets, are pulling the trench close to her body, and she's slightly hunched against the chill of the gray London day. She isn't wearing anything special, no couture or ostrich feathers or over-the-knee boots. Her hair is windblown, and we can see a glimpse of a skirt and sweater beneath the coat. She's just a girl out for a walk on a blustery afternoon—except that she's as radiant as the sun and as mysterious as the Mona Lisa. Shrimpton is gazing straight into the camera, but she has an unknowable quality. She looks like a woman with secrets.

According to Coco Chanel, this is a quality that all women should cultivate. "A woman's unhappiness is to rely on her youth," she once said. "Youth must be replaced by mystery." Though Shrimpton is just a teenager in this photo, she's obviously absorbed Chanel's advice. But even the most studious pupil needs props. Shrimpton is wearing hers: A trusty trench coat, fashion's most mysterious garment.

Perennially popular with stage and screen detectives and spies, the trench is inscrutability incarnate. Its traditional sand beige color is sedate, its design resolutely functional—this is a coat that gives nothing away. It's the outdoor garb of the businessman, the least showy creature in the human menagerie. Yet when it comes to creating an aura of allure, the trench coat is unparalleled. Black lace bras and garter belts have nothing on a tightly cinched trench. They're so obvious, all spilling flesh and exposed curves. A trench, on the other hand, makes you want to work to have a look at what's underneath—anything with that many fastenings is just begging to be undone. It's sexy, but it's subtle. When the editors of *In Style* wanted to reinforce the parallels they were drawing between the wholesome country singer Faith Hill and the hard-living, sexually omnivorous French chanteuse Edith Piaf (whom Hill professes to love in an accompanying article), they posed Hill not in slinky black but in a white trench and knee-high stiletto boots. She'd look forced in the former, while the latter brushes her with a tint of danger.

Though the trench coat is never out of style, its popularity ebbs and flows. It's one of those items of clothing that suffers from occasional perceptions of dowdiness—visions of the Queen in a headscarf and a Burberry, a pack of corgis yapping at her ankles come to mind—only to rebound chicer than ever. The reason for the trench coat's enduring appeal is simple: It's one of the most enigmatic, flattering, high-status things you can slip into. And unlike a ballgown or sky-high heels, you can wear a trench almost anywhere without feeling out of place. Whether you're running out for coffee and the paper, a job interview, or a late-night drink, a trench makes sense. As a bonus, it adds an undercurrent of drama to any situation without being in the least bit costumey. A trench evokes images of Humphrey Bogart nobly saying good-bye to Ingrid Bergman in the last few minutes of *Casablanca*. It's like the forty-league boots or other magic garments found in fairy tales, a ticket into a world more exotic than your own, in which a trip to the corner store for milk can take on some of the romance of a journey to North Africa to bid farewell to a lover who will make any sacrifice for you.

With all this romance you get practicality. The trench coat is a serious garment, meant to protect the wearer against the elements. When foreign correspondents file their reports from war zones, they're apt to be wearing trenches (one, Knowlton Nash, titled his autobiography *History on the Run: The Trenchcoat Memoirs of a Foreign Correspondent*). They know its air of authority adds to the weight of their words. This tactic isn't limited to up-and-comers in the field. Journalists who've made the jump to network anchor seem to keep one in their closets for those times when they're called on to go out into the streets; if Dan Rather is "live" anywhere, you can be sure he's wearing a trench.

You're never at risk of looking trite in a trench coat. It's a garment that means business. But it's this very nature—covered-up, self-contained—that makes the trench so transgressively sexy. You may look all buttoned up when you're wearing one, but underneath you could be any number of things: improper, disheveled, even naked. This tension is heightened by the very proper color of the trench. Beige and tan are, according to Alison Lurie in *The Language of Clothes,* "the most neutral of all colors, the least communicative . . . In itself, tan is neither cheerful nor sad, active nor passive. People who prefer to conceal their emotions, or must do so for professional reasons, often wear outfits that are largely or entirely tan or beige." In effect, a trench coat is urban armor, protection against the prying eyes of one's fellow citizens. Wear one and you look law-abiding and inoffensive. (A black trench conveys just the opposite impression: It can look as sinister as Dracula's cape, particularly if it's cut from a high-tech fabric. In the 1999 film *The Matrix*, a high-tech sci-fi thriller that pitted Keanu Reeves and friends against a computer-generated menace, Reeves and company were shrouded in black trench coats, which, despite their good-guy status, made them appear menacing. The black trench looks hostile, an image that was reinforced when, the same year that *The Matrix* was released, two high school students who were members of a clique known as The Trench Coat Mafia—because of their black trenches—killed twelve people in Littleton, Colorado, before turning their guns on themselves.)

No wonder it's the classic choice of the flasher. With a cover-up that respectable, who would ever expect what was in store? Marc Jacobs riffed on this theme in his fall 2002 ads, which showed the actress Asia Argento posing with her baby. In the first frame, Argento is shown leaning toward the stroller that holds the baby, playfully clutching her tan trench coat closed; in the next, she's holding the trench wide open, revealing what looks like a vintage camisole and step-ins, underwear so charmingly demure and old-fashioned that you have to smile. That same season, Prada added a kinky edge to the trench by cutting it from clear plastic. In their ad, a model is posed with one foot up on a chair and a hand on her hip, wearing nothing but the transparent trench and high-heel black pumps. With her strictly pulled back hair, she looks like a very high-end dominatrix.

The Prada ad is extreme, but the juxtaposition of masculine details (all those buckles and buttons) and the femininity of a minute, belted waist is hard to resist. As Kristina Richards observed in the November 2002 issue of *Harper's Bazaar*, "A belted coat will give almost anyone an hourglass figure, which is why trenches are such a staple in women's wardrobes across the board." I have a trench made of distressed, heavyweight leather, rather like an old-fashioned aviator's coat. It's cut with a wide, swingy skirt, and when the belt's pulled in tight, the silhouette is very New Look. It sways slightly when I walk, bringing to mind images of Christian Dior's full-skirted *elegantes.* The lived-in leather, on the other hand, is as tough looking as an old boot. The juxtaposition is very satisfying.

The classy sexiness of the trench has its roots in the coat's origins: war. Because waging war is a high-status pursuit, the clothes associated with it are invariably prestigious. The long list of attire with a military background includes ties, which are descended from the tight-fitting cravats worn by Croatian mercenaries during the Thirty Years' War (1618–48); the blazer, first sported by officers on the British warship H.M.S. *Blazer* in the 1860s; the Wellington boot, developed by the Duke of Wellington during the Napoleonic Wars (1796–1815); khakis, initially donned by British soldiers in India during the nineteenth century (the name is derived from the Hindi word for dust—khakis were a sort of urcamouflage) to replace their scarlet wool tunics; button-down shirts, whose collars were also devised by nineteenth-century Britons in the Subcontinent, so that the pointed ends wouldn't flap in their faces while they played polo (a game they had recently invented to while away the off-hours in India); and the wristwatch, popularized by British officers during World War I, when it was realized that checking the time was more easily accomplished by thrusting out a wrist rather than fumbling for a pocket watch in an interior pocket. All these garments and accessories are associated with old-line, upper-class tastes. War may no longer be the game of aristocrats, but the mystique of the warrior endures.

World War I, the same conflict that gave us trench warfare and trench foot, saw the introduction of the trench coat. Once again, the British were behind this innovation. The new coat was intended to keep officers dry and warm in the trenches, hence the name. To this end, pretty much every part of the trench coat was designed with an eye to the utilitarian. It was made from a waterproof fabric called gabardine and cut generously enough to be used as a blanket. The double-breasted fastenings provided extra coverage, and the wool lining was removable so the coat could be worn year-round. The epaulets unbuttoned to secure a rifle strap, and the belt loops were equipped with brass D-rings that could be used as grenade hooks (something to think of next time you buckle up). The separate shoulder yoke and gun flap functioned like the rain fly on a tent, deflecting water and keeping the underlying layer of fabric dry. The voluminous pockets were large enough to hold maps, provisions, and extra ammunition. The wool-lined collar could be turned-up and the buckles around the wrist could be tightened to keep out the rain. Many of these details, though vestigial, can still be found in a modern trench. They add to its glamour—there's something thrilling about putting on a coat that hasn't changed in ninety years, especially when its original design was so heroically conceived. Even a new trench is steeped in history.

The coats were made for the British army by Burberry, a hallowed name in trench-coat lore. Humphrey Bogart, the patron saint of the trench, wore a Burberry, as did Audrey Hepburn. A Burberry trench is the quintessential trench coat. In fact, by 1924, the year that the company's signature camel plaid lining was introduced, all trench coats were generically known as burberrys.

The firm of Burberry was founded in 1856 by twenty-one-year-old Thomas Burberry, a country draper's apprentice. That year, Burberry struck out on his own, opening an outfitter's shop in rural Hampshire, England. The shop supplied the locals and visiting sportsmen with outdoor clothes and equipment. The business grew steadily over the next fourteen years, but it was in 1880, when Burberry developed the textile he named gabardine, that things really took off. His goal was to create a fabric which would keep country doctors dry as they made house calls in inclement weather. Primitive water-resistant fabrics existed, but they didn't breathe, which made wearing them disagreeable, and they smelled strongly of rubber. Burberry's innovation was to treat the yarn with a secret waterproofing process before it was woven into fabric, which resulted in a breathable cloth that was both durable and waterproof. The first raincoat made of this new fabric was produced in the late 1890s, and was an immediate hit. As one satisfied customer from Perthshire wrote to Thomas Burberry, "Without my Burberry outdoor life in this country would be misery." The company's reputation for making outdoor gear was so high that it outfitted several polar and Himalayan expeditions, including Captain Roald Amundsen's triumphant 1911 journey to the

South Pole. Amundsen left behind his Burberry gabardine tent to inform his competitor in the race to reach the pole, Captain Robert Falcon Scott, that he had gotten there first.

Burberry had already been supplying the British army for years when it was called on in 1914 to adapt its raincoat to the rigors of life in the trenches. The result was equally popular with the public and with soldiers, and by the early 1920s, trench coats were a common sight on city streets. Burberry made products other than trenches, and lots of other companies—most notably Aquascutum, which also claims ownership of the trench, citing a raincoat produced for British troops during the Crimean War (1853–56)—made trenches, but over the years Burberry and the trench became inextricably linked. However, by the mid-1990s, the company image had gotten a little fusty. Designers had seized on the trench in the late 1960s, cutting it slimmer and sleeker than the traditional, flapping Burberry model. The dependable Burberry trench was associated with middle-aged businessmen, and the prestige of the brand had been seriously undermined with a series of dubious licensing deals (Burberry whiskey anyone?). Burberry's, as the company name had become, decided it was time for an overhaul. With a new CEO and a new designer at the helm, Burberry set out to court the world's fashion arbiters. First off, the original name was restored. Next, the venerable camel-colored plaid was made into such unsportsmanlike items as teeny bikinis and strappy stiletto sandals. Hip British models Kate Moss and Stella Tennant were recruited to pose for ads. A new collection, Burberry Prorsum (Latin for forward, *prorsum* is the Burberry motto) was launched and pushed the brand's sportswear heritage into the foreground of fashion. Most recently, Burberry started a made-to-order business. Customers willing to wait six weeks for the prestige of a custom-made trench can now have one tailored to their exact specifications. Writing in *Vogue* in November 2002, the self-described "horribly demanding, superspoiled, and very difficult" Plum Sykes professed herself delighted at the opportunity to apply the exactness of haute couture to the illustrious lineage of British sportswear: "You could say that I consider the Burberry trench to be the only mackintosh that can be described as an icon. The idea that I could have one tailored for me by English tailors was, well, fashion heaven." Not surprisingly, Sykes chose not to alter the Burberry's classic lines. As she astutely observed, "Why take the heart out of a legend?"

Today, though it has given up none of its historic credentials, Burberry is certifiably hip. Indeed, the company's storied heritage is part of the Burberry mystique. Among trendsetters such as actress Chloë Sevigny and her chum Tara Subkoff, the designer of the subversive Imitation of Christ clothing line, a vintage Burberry dating from before the brand's renaissance is the thing to have. This distinction confirms the wearer's status as a woman who has always been cool, and therefore able to identify a cult label long before anyone else. This kind of oneupmanship is the ne plus ultra of "What, this old thing? I've had it forever."

Though I don't have a trusty, decades-old Burberry mellowing in my closet, trench and trench-type coats form the basis of my outdoor wardrobe. If describing the number of coats and jackets I have as a wardrobe sounds extensive, it's meant to. I have a lot of coats. I think this is because I grew up in a cold climate—in primary school in Montreal, my classmates and I recited a poem by the French-Canadian poet Roch Carrier that includes the line *Mon pays, c'est l'hiver* (My country is winter)—and, consequently, wore some sort of coat or jacket for most of the year. Having a wide selection of outerwear to choose from makes me feel as though my options are open, and fends off the boredom that comes from wearing the same coat for seven dreary months.

Though I also have wrap coats and pea coats and car coats, the trench is the outerwear style I return to again and again. Apart from the leather New Look number, I have a red corduroy one, a dark wool, and the traditional pale beige lined in plaid. In a trench, I feel ready for anything, secure in the comfort that no matter what happens, I look neat and pulled-together. Maybe it's the action of pulling the belt tight that brings on this feeling of serene preparedness. It's a way of girding yourself—literally—for battle.

Hollywood invested in the imagery of the trench early on. In 1928, the great West Coast costumer and designer Adrian put Greta Garbo in a slouch hat and plaid-lined trench for their first film together, *A Woman of Affairs.* It cemented Garbo's reputation as a remote, mysterious figure. Women loved the look, and it was widely copied. By the 1940s, when Humphrey Bogart emerged as the definitive trench-coat wearer, it was a widely recognized symbol of the private eye. The trench gave Bogey and the other stars who wore it an aura of heroic glamour. This technique was especially effective in film noir, where the trench coat's clean-looking color was a foil for the darkness of the city. In *Phantom Lady,* a classic of this genre released in 1944, Ella Raines, playing a secretary trying to clear her boss of a murder charge, trails a reluctant witness through the late-night streets of Manhattan, her white trench coat glowing like a beacon of hope.

But Hollywood's best-known female trench wearers were the two Hepburns: Katharine and Audrey. Katharine Hepburn favored trench coats to top her masculine ensembles, and she wore them with a rakish charm. In a photo taken on a movie set in the 1940s, she's wearing jeans, a black sweater, dark socks, and espadrilles, topped off with a light beige trench. She looks stylish in an offbeat, very modern way—or at least she does to me. At the time Katharine Hepburn's style was considered mannish and unsuitable, and studio bosses were always after her to wear something a little more feminine. They had no complaints, however, about the gamine charm of Audrey Hepburn, who assured the continued popularity of the trench coat by making it de rigueur for any teenage girl aspiring to her beatnik grace. In both *Sabrina* (1954) and *Funny Face* (1957) she wears a trench before being transformed into a high-fashion goddess in Paris; she recreated the trench-over-black look in *Breakfast at Tiffany's* (1961). Very few teens could afford to wear Givenchy, Hepburn's chosen couturier, but her pre-Paris wardrobe was well within reach. Writes Ellen Melnikoff in *What We Wore*, "Black tights, black turtleneck, and a trench coat—that's what we wanted to wear to knock around in, even though we were doing our knocking around in Levittown instead of the Left Bank. Audrey may have preferred the creations of Givenchy in her private life, but she made the beatnik look respectable, workable, elegant."

Audrey's trench was a piece of sartorial foreshadowing, a hint of the impeccable taste and refinement she was to show in her couture reincarnation. A trench coat has noble associations—by wearing it in a seemingly artless way, Audrey was playing the part of the diamond in the rough, in want of only a little polishing to shine with a rare brilliance. Had she strolled along the Seine in a black leather jacket, the image would have been quite different. A latter-day example of the class-giving power of the trench is Madonna, who in her guise as an upper-middle-class Englishwoman has taken to wearing one.

Along with defining the high-class beatnik look, Audrey Hepburn provided Hollywood with a convenient shorthand for identifying off-beat female characters, thanks to her *Funny Face* role as a vaguely artsy bookstore clerk who eccentrically scorns high fashion for the study of "empathicalism." Audiences soon recognized any woman wearing a black sweater and a trench on-screen as free-sprited—sometimes fatally so. In *The Best of Everything,* a 1959 film about a trio of office pals and their romances, model Suzy Parker plays the most artistic of the friends, the one who aspires to the stage. Sure enough, she slinks around in a trench and a black sweater. It's the outfit she's wearing when she accidentally plunges to her death while stalking a disinterested lover. Fourteen years later, in *The Way We Were,* Barbra Streisand wears a similar outfit. The film, about the romance and ultimately doomed marriage of a feisty, politically minded, working-class Jewish girl (Streisand) and a privileged WASP (Robert Redford), spans the 1930s to the late 1950s. The characters are reunited for a moment at the end, in front of the Plaza Hotel in New York. Redford, in a suit, is squiring a country-club blonde into the Oak Bar. The frizzy-haired Streisand is attending a political rally wearing—what else?—a black turtleneck and a beige trench. The trench is still a potent symbol of bohemianism: In Baz Luhrman's recent Broadway production of *La Bohème*, set in the 1950s, Mimi, the original beatnik, wore a trench.

Across the Atlantic, Audrey's bohemian chic caught the eye of an English art student named Barbara Hulanicki, who later used her as the prototype for the skinny, faunlike Biba girl. The early Biba art student look, which included a black sweater, a short jumper, and, of course, a trench, was a classic look of the early 1960s.

With the advent of the mini, the trench got abbreviated. In 1971's *Klute* Jane Fonda wore her miniscule tan trench with thigh-high black boots, mixing short and long, propriety and naughtiness. It was a juxtaposition that reflected the character she portrayed, the brittle, streetwise prostitute Bree Daniels.

More recently, a trench coat was worn by the French actress Charlotte Gainsbourg in *Ma femme est une actrice*. Portraying an actress whose husband thinks she's having an affair, Gainsbourg lopes around London in her own classic beige trench accessorized with a handknit hat and muffler. She looks smashing and manages to be thoroughly modern without disregarding the trench's historic spirit, both insouciant and iconic. In wearing her trench with such off-hand chic, Gainsbourg is following a long French tradition. Though the trench was not intended to be a fashion item, it has been championed by many designers, most notably the Frenchmen Yves Saint Laurent and Jean Paul Gaultier.

Saint Laurent, who first showed a trench coat in 1968, continued to put them on his runway throughout his long career. In his hands the trench was rendered more fluid and sensual than its British prototype. Saint Laurent cut his trench closer to the body, thereby drawing out its innate sexiness. On the runway, he paired it with high heels and other symbols of femininity. He made the coat a wardrobe staple in the early 1970s, a symbol of the chic, liberated woman.

Jean Paul Gaultier, on the other hand, has mined the trench coat legend for its more outré possibilities. Gaultier can certainly cut a mean everyday trench, but he excels at fantastic interpretations of its venerable lines. In his fall 1998 couture collection he included a full-length, trench coat-styled evening gown. Cut from navy blue wool, it hugged the torso and fanned out into a train, emphasizing the curve of the figure with two rows of buttons. A matching bolero jacket stood in for the shoulder flap and epaulettes. Its trailing, trumpet-shaped sleeves framed the waist, which was made to look even tinier by the flare of the jacket. Two years later, Gaultier sent out a swimsuit that was styled in the manner of a typical beige trench: double-breasted and wrapped tightly at the throat. In Gaultier's beguilingly off-kilter worldview, the fact that both garments are worn around water is reason enough to combine them.

In the past few years, the trench coat has been rediscovered by a new generation of wearers. Designers ranging from Marc Jacobs to Oscar de la Renta have put trenches on their runways, often personalizing them with brightly colored fabrics or asymmetrical closures. Countless magazines have trumpeted it as a "classic" without which every wardrobe is bereft. When I walk down the street in New York, I see women of all ages wearing them and I have to say, I approve mightily. They look sleek and a little mischevious, like heiresses running errands for the heck of it. Indeed, I think the current vogue for the trench has something to do with fuzzy childhood memories of watching Audrey Hepburn films on television. More than forty years after most of them were made, she continues to inspire imitation. Writing in *The New York Times Magazine* in the fall of 2002, Caitlin Macy noted, "What most young women are left with after seeing *Breakfast at Tiffany's* is a desire to live in Manhattan and be madcap." Among the must-have accoutrements of the madcap, Macy goes on to say, is "a classic Burberry raincoat," just like Holly Golightly wore. Much has been made of the black Givenchy shift Hepburn wore in the film, and rightly so. But the image that remains with me is from the final scenes, when a flustered Hepburn dashes out of a cab and into a heavy downpour in search of the cat she had abandoned just minutes before. She's wearing her trench coat, and though she's on the verge of hysteria, she looks fabulous. I can't settle into a cab on a rainy day without thinking of her.

Lipstick

"Darling," she instructed me, "would you reach in that drawer there and give me my purse. A girl doesn't read this sort of thing without her lipstick."

—Truman Capote

THE LAST THING I DO BEFORE LEAVING THE HOUSE IN the morning is put on lipstick. That done, the line between my private and public selves is drawn and I'm ready for the street. Now, I'm no beauty buff. In fact, my entire cosmetics collection consists of lipstick and its kissing cousin, lip balm. I have salves that soften, glosses that shine, creams that protect, and tints that darken. I've amassed a sizable collection in my quest for the Holy Grail of cosmetics: The Perfect Lipstick. My requirements are really quite simple: The color must be a sheer, *slightly* brown (but not *too* brown) red, with a hint of berry to it. It must look natural rather than clownish. The consistency must be light and very faintly slick. Finally, it must be emollient and last long enough to make frequent reapplication unnecessary.

What is it about lipstick that makes even a woman who is apathetic to other forms of makeup so passionate about it? Well, for one thing, lipstick is easy—with minimum effort you can achieve maximum impact. It looks great on an otherwise bare face, and there's no need to guess about where to apply it. Makeup artists suggest using liner and a brush for greater precision, but most women follow the modus operandi described by Elizabeth McCracken, a self-confessed lipstick addict, in the June 1997 issue of *Allure*: "Do I use lipliner? Did van Gogh paint by numbers? I don't cotton to any of those lipstick niceties. I just whip out the stick, twirl it up, and slap it on." In the 1930s, *Vogue* dubbed this one of the signature gestures of the twentieth century. In fact, women have worn some form of lip color for thousands of years—sticks of ocher have been found in tombs that date back to 5000 B.C.E. But before the first commercial tube went on sale in 1915, color was dabbed on with a finger or painted on with a brush. The tube came into being just as women were making their mark: getting the vote, entering the professions, and graduating from universities. Pulling out your tube and swiping on a lick of color became a way of asserting your independence. It's still a thrilling gesture, though not seen as often as it was in lipstick's infancy. In her introduction to *Read My Lips: A Cultural History of Lipstick,* Véronique Vienne calls for the reinstatement of this public thrill by trying to convince her friends that a flaunted lipstick is a form of feminine power: "Imagine fancy restaurants full of ladies-who-lunch wagging their uncapped Borghese and Chanel lipsticks . . . one can't help but watch in anticipation. When they do speak . . . the world will be all ears."

But the appeal of lipstick goes deeper than the ease and satisfaction of its application. It's a cosmetic that packs a powerful psychological punch—putting it on can transform your mood. "When a woman has lost her lover, when a girl has lost her job, when the doctor has told his fatal news, when the luck is leaving, the dinner party flopping, the birth pains beginning, the scandal breaking, the storm striking, the other woman sailing by in triumph . . . the sudden streak of lipstick across the lips spells courage," was the somewhat melodramatic conclusion *Harper's Bazaar* came to in 1946. In her autobiography, *My Life for Beauty,* Helena Rubinstein refers to an even more extreme case. She tells a story of a woman being carried out of a bombed-out London building during the Blitz. She was quite badly injured, but before agreeing to take any medication, she asked for her lipstick, explaining, "It does something for me."

This hearkens back to the original role of face and body paint: that of protective charm. Archaeologists theorize that applying makeup was originally a way of attracting friendly spirits and discouraging malevolent ones. Even as makeup came to be seen as more of an enhancement than a talisman, its appearance was becoming quite ritualized.

For the past two thousand years, the primary purpose of lipstick has been to enhance the looks of the wearer. In our society, lipstick is worn only by women (though this wasn't always so; like the high heel, lipstick has at times been a unisex accessory) so it carries certain sexual associations. Though male and female infants and children alike have fairly full, intensely pigmented lips, hormonal changes bring an end to this similarity at puberty, when boys' lips thin out and girls' lips curve and swell. The sexes attract one another by emphasizing what makes them different, which is why men cultivate muscular physiques and women wear low-cut tops. By darkening her lips, a woman makes them look even lusher than they already are. Men with very red lips are often a little unsettling, because they confound our ideas about sexuality.

The pneumatic, rosy lip is also a sign of youth and the ability to bear children. As women age, their lips tend to get thinner and lose some of their color. Lipstick can be interpreted as an attempt to look fresh and ever-ripe. (Collagen is another option, albeit a costly and painful one.) In the September 2002 issue of *Harper's Bazaar*, makeup artist Charlie Green suggests adding a dab of clear gloss to the center of the lower lip. "This creates a sort of optical illusion—a sexy 3-D effect—and gives you that full, poufy Lolita lip," she explains. "There's nothing better than lips that look big and sexy, but natural, too."

More explicitly, Diane Ackerman, the author of *A Natural History of the Senses*, tells us that ". . . the lips remind us of the labia, because they flush red and swell when they're aroused, which is the conscious or subconscious reason women have always made them look even redder with lipstick." Writing about red lipstick for the August 1994 issue of *Vogue*, Julia Reed reports that a man guesses that she is in love by the shade of her mouth. "'. . . it's darker,' he said. 'Redder, more defined.'"

(Interestingly, most lipsticks are scented with vanilla, a fragrance that both men and women find pleasing, and one that reinforces lipstick's candylike appeal. But the sexual frisson of darkened lips and the homey smell of freshly baked cookies make for an odd juxtaposition.)

However, I would guess that for many women lipstick isn't sexual but feminine. Like most women, my introduction to lipstick came via my mother. I have vivid memories of her leaning toward the bathroom mirror, gliding color onto her lips. I would linger in the doorway, watching; I felt I was observing a ritual that I would one day be initiated into. When she clicked the tube shut, it was a signal that we were about to leave the house. My mother kept her makeup in a white wicker basket—the bottom half of a purse some kind but misguided family friend had given me—in the medicine cabinet. I loved rummaging through its contents: palettes of iridescent blue, Cover Girl eye shadow (this was the '70s), flat pans of creamy blush, mascara, and, best of all, coral-colored lipsticks (in her defense, I must say that my mother is a natural golden blonde and so looks quite spectacular in coral lipstick—and again, this was the '70s). To my five-year-old self, lipstick was the very essence of femininity. And to this day, I don't swivel my lipstick open without hearing my mother warning me not to swivel it all the way—so enticing to me in advertisements—because the bullet of color will break off.

The idea of lipstick as the key to the meaning of womanhood has been the subject of many female artists' work. Janine Antoni, for example, uses lipstick to explore topics such as beauty and self-image. For *Diary*, she wore one hundred different lipstick shades for each of one hundred different daily activities. The used lipsticks were then displayed as a diary of her life during this period. As part of a work called *Gnaw*, Antoni chewed on a large block of lard for several months, collected the bits she spat out, and shaped them into lipsticks. The lipsticks were then arranged in a cosmetics counter-style case, opposite the chewed-on block of lard.

The photographer Stacey Greene takes a more straightforward approach—she documents the used lipsticks of friends, acquaintances, and strangers to illustrate how mass-made objects take on personal meaning. Though lipstick has come in approximately three shapes—all variations on the bullet—since the late 1930s, every women puts it on slightly differently, resulting in thousands of different shapes, some flat, others wildly asymmetrical. Just as lipstick makes its mark on women, so women make their mark on lipstick.

On-screen, lipstick is often equated with femininity, especially dangerous femininity. In *La femme Nikita,* the preternaturally feminine Jeanne Moreau, playing an instructor in a secret-agent training program, attempts to pass on some of her expertise to the feral trainee, Anne Parillaud, by teaching her how to put on lipstick. "Let your pleasure be your guide," she intones. "Your pleasure as a woman. And don't forget . . . there are two things that have no limit: femininity and the means of taking advantage of it." What Moreau is teaching is how to be a femme fatale, and in the movies at least, a femme fatale is never without her lipstick—no matter what state she's in. For example, in *The Postman Always Rings Twice,* femme fatale Lana Turner makes novel use of her lipstick to attract John Garfield's attention: She rolls it across the floor to his feet. She subsequently persuades Garfield to kill her husband, winning him over by cooing, "You'll think of something—you're smart." Later in the film, she's killed in a car crash. Our last view of her is a limp arm hanging out the window of the wrecked car, a lipstick clutched in its lifeless hand. It's a bad end for a bad woman.

Though the film is in black and white, I would bet that Turner's lipstick was red, the quintessential choice of the femme fatale. Red is associated with blood, passion, vitality, desire, and aggression. In literature and drama, red is an indicator of strong sexuality. Blanche Dubois, the nymphomaniac sister in *A Streetcar Named Desire,* wears a prim white suit and pearls in public, but a slatternly red kimono in private. In *Jezebel,* Bette Davis, playing a spoiled, headstrong southern belle, rebelliously wears a red dress to her coming-out ball.

Sexual undertones aside, wearing red lipstick carries a certain responsibility. It's a color that requires constant vigilance and upkeep—nothing looks worse than faded and smeared red lipstick. You can't be laissez-faire about a scarlet mouth. If you're going to paint your lips red, they will be the center of attention, so you better have something to say. Two of the crimson mouth's most famous representatives were Coco Chanel and Diana Vreeland, neither of whom was ever at a loss for words. Perhaps just knowing that you're wearing red can summon chutzpah. "It gives me confidence. It's so aggressive, you have to follow," one red-lipped woman reported about her lipstick choice in the August 1994 issue of *Vogue*.

At the other end of the lipstick scale, pink is a less intense version of red—the femininity minus the sizzle, the color baby girls are traditionally assigned. According to Anne Marie Iverson, the former beauty director of *Harper's Bazaar*, men like their girlfriends to wear red, but prefer their wives in pink.

In the nineteenth century, when any form of makeup was taboo, a woman who wore lipstick was considered sexually available. Even when makeup became generally accepted, it retained many subtle symbolic nuances. A woman with a crimson mouth was a siren; one who chose a paler, more subdued pink lipstick was a nice girl. But the nice-girl category is a confining one—given a choice between red and pink lipstick, women will often go for red, as the cosmetics maker Volupté learned in 1938. That year, the company launched two shades of lipstick, one a red called Hussy, the other a pink called Lady. According to Kathy Peiss, author of *Hope in a Jar: The Making of America's Beauty Culture*, Hussy outsold Lady five to one. Even today, pink lipsticks are given sweet, innocent sounding names such as Debutante, Barely There, and Blush. Reds, on the other hand, get dangerous-sounding monikers: Shanghai Express, Rouge Diabolique, Decadence.

No one today holds up lipstick as a symbol of immorality; faced with the sight of starlets such as Britney Spears stripping down to simulated nudity on national television, we've gotten relatively blasé about makeup. No one blinked an eye when M·A·C had RuPaul and k.d. lang (a drag queen and a lesbian, respectively) pose for their ads for Viva Glam lipstick, the proceeds of which go to the M·A·C AIDS Fund. But for almost as long as women have painted their lips and faces, moralists have found something to be outraged about. Most often, the complaint was centered around the "false face" that lipstick and other cosmetics created. In some cases, this was held to be an offense against God. The early Christians, living among makeup-mad Romans, scorned any hint of artificial color as a sin. But throughout history, a far more common complaint about lipstick—indeed, about any cosmetic—was that it created a false bill of goods. Men who married women they took to be rosy-lipped and dewy-cheeked became indignant when the artifice behind their wives' "natural" beauty was revealed. In 1963, in *Sex and the Single Girl*, Helen Gurley Brown described a friend who got up early every morning to put on what sounds like a fair amount of makeup: foundation, eyeliner, mascara, and lipstick. The reason for this predawn secrecy? Her obviously clueless husband liked to brag that his wife didn't wear makeup.

Humans have decorated their faces and bodies for millennia. Cosmetics have been found in tombs that are more than five thousand years old, and it is quite probable that staining the lips with berries or ocher goes back even further. The Egyptians, both male and female, were adept cosmeticians—they were even buried with containers of lip rouge (made from henna and carmine) and kohl eyeliner so they would look good in the afterlife. Roman women favored red-tinted ocher, iron or fucus, a type of algae, to color their lips, while their Greek sisters used vermilion. A medieval poet praised lips that were "plump and redder than cochineal," a dye made from ground-up insects that is still a popular lipstick colorant, only now it's called carmine.

Lip painting was popular throughout the Renaissance, when the sought-after effect was a stark white face—usually obtained with some form of poisonous lead-based paste—and scarlet lips. Elizabeth I of England was a fan of this look.

When she died, she reportedly had half an inch of paint on her face.

The red-and-white look was popular with the upper classes until the French Revolution—in 1789, the year the trumbulls first rolled through the streets of Paris, about 2 million pots of rouge were purchased in France. Along with complicated, oversized hairdos and dangling lace cuffs, the red-and-white face was abandoned after the Revolution in favor of a more natural look. Women continued to paint, but more subtly. Men gave it up altogether, and haven't touched it since—at least not publicly.

With the new emphasis on natural beauty, any sort of enhancement was looked on with suspicion. Guerlain sold lip balm as early as 1828, and women continued to mix up lip salves and other skincare items at home, but any hint of artificial color was discouraged. Magazines such as *Godey's Lady's Book*, a favorite of nineteenth-century American women, portrayed rouge and powder as dangerous temptations of urban life, best avoided by any woman who wished to retain her good reputation. Visible color was associated with prostitutes and actresses (who were considered no better than the former). Fashionable society women also colored their lips and cheeks, though they were less likely to admit to doing so. Consequently, "Did she or didn't she?" was a favorite topic of gossip. But even women who didn't dare experiment with rouge tried to imitate its effect—some sucked on cinnamon drops, while others bit their lips or rubbed moistened red crepe paper or satin ribbon on them.

It wasn't until the 1890s that lipstick began to win back some of the ground it had lost to Victorian prudishness. Peiss quotes a *New York World* headline of 1890: "Society women now paint . . . even in the very best circles." By 1897, even the venerable Sears catalog was selling rouge described as a "harmless preparation for giving color to the lips and cheeks," for fifty cents a pot. By 1915, with the introduction of the sliding metal tube, lipstick had assumed the shape familiar to us today.

Despite assertions by Sears and other retailers and manufacturers that their cosmetics were harmless, many were not. Until Congress passed the federal Food, Drug, and Cosmetics Act in 1938, there were no laws governing the production of makeup or the sorts of claims manufacturers might boast of. Lead, aniline dyes, and other dangerous chemicals were used. Today, all lipsticks sold in the United Sates must indicate the specific colorants on the packaging. Colorants are always the last ingredients listed and are followed by the letters FD&C or D&C, to indicate that they've been approved by the Food and Drug Administration.

In 1923, when an estimated 50 million American women were wearing lipstick without the benefit of the FDA, an alarmed James H. Collins wrote an article for the *Saturday Evening Post* that raised the possibility of mass poisoning. Collins, however, was not concerned about the women wearing the lipstick, but about all the men those women were kissing. Worried about his claims, the New York Board of Health considered banning lipstick, though the idea was quickly dropped as impractical.

The 1920s were when lipstick really came into its own. In 1920, Max Factor, who had run a professional makeup studio for film and stage actors since 1909, launched Society

Makeup, a line of cosmetics intended for everyday use. Factor was inspired to create the line when he realized that women were adapting his theatrical makeup for street wear. Scores of other cosmetics lines were launched in the '20s. By 1925, the American cosmetics industry was spending millions of dollars per year on advertising—only food and beverage manufacturers shelled out more to push their products.

Lipstick could be had for as little as a dime in the 1920s, putting it well within the reach of the working girl. Colors tended toward the garish and were applied enthusiastically rather than expertly. As the fashion critic Bernadine Morris wrote in *Vogue* in 1976, "Women were just beginning to wear makeup then and they didn't quite know how to go about it." Period novels such as *The Green Hat,* which was published in 1924, describe fashionable characters with lips as "scarlet as the inside of a pome-granate," or "purple in the dim light" against skin powdered "gardenia-white."

This look had become passé by the 1930s, a time when advertisers began emphasizing the naturalness of lipstick and other cosmetics. By natural, they meant that as long as one made some effort to match the color of one's lipstick to one's complexion, then one was enhancing one's looks, not falsifying them. Consequently, beauty writers counseled against applying lipstick in public, which would nullify the illusion of naturalness. Makeup colors began to be coordinated with fashions, and new colors were released seasonally. "NEW! . . . As new as a Paris fashion cable! As red-red as the stripe in the blouse sketched here!" enthused one late-'30s ad for Dorothy Gray lipstick. Women were urged to look good all the time, by taking care to coordinate their lipstick to their activities. "No matter where you are this summer . . . on the beach, the golf links, or dining and dancing . . . fashion says you must look *glamorous!"* declared a 1939 ad for Du Barry cosmetics.

Very few women could afford to look glamorous during the Depression. Lipstick was one of the few affordable luxuries, so that a woman who wasn't wearing any was seen as really hard up. My grandmother, who came of age in the 1930s, wouldn't dream of appearing on the street without it. Before going to visit her, my mother would always put on lipstick. I remember sitting in the car with her in front of my grandparents' house, as she pulled a tube out of her purse, saying, "I had better put on some lipstick or grandma will think I don't feel well."

The 1940s were red-letter days for lipstick. Taboos against cosmetics had virtually disappeared, and the idea that a woman "put on her face" as a way of expressing her personality was widely accepted, at least among the young. By 1941, American women were spending $20 million a year on lipstick. Even World War II didn't slow down consumption. Although it was briefly placed on the rationed list, this ruling was quickly rescinded—lipstick, authorities realized, was good for morale. In Britain, the government wasn't so enlightened; lipstick production in the United Kingdom was suspended for the duration of the war, a move that led to a flourishing black market.

Doing men's jobs made women feel like they had to work harder at being feminine. Women had never earned such high wages before, and men felt threatened. By looking as fetching as possible—not always easy to do in the canvas boilersuits and hair-covering turbans that many war workers had to wear—women sought to reassure men that their traditional role of breadwinner had not been usurped. Editorials and advertising promoted glamour as a virtue, one of the things that the boys overseas were defending. The cosmetics and fragrance manufacturer Coty sponsored the Women's Military Services Club in New York. Tangee, one of the biggest lipstick makers of the time, launched a campaign called War, Women and Lipstick. "No lipstick—ours or anyone else's—will win the war. But it symbolizes one of the reasons we are fighting . . . the precious right of women to be feminine and lovely, under any circumstances," was one example of the copy that accompanied the ads. Even women on the frontlines clung to their lipstick: It was one of the few personal possessions that evacuated navy nurses took with them. Formerly the badge of loose women, lipstick had become a symbol of American values.

To bolster the patriotic image, lipstick shades were rechristened to suggest valor rather than sex: Jeep Red, Commando, and Fighting Red were typical names. Not that love and romance were forgotten: A World War II–era ad for Tussy brand lipstick offered tips on recognizing officer insignia—why flirt with a private when there's a captain in the room is the suggestion—under the heading, HE LOST HIS HEART TO A PAIR OF ROSY LIPS.

Lipstick was even more popular after the war. In 1946, American women had upped their annual spending on it to $30 million. According to *Life*, this was enough to pay the president's salary for seventy-seven years. In the 1950s, one survey found that 99.7 percent of college girls owned a lipstick; another discovered that 98 percent of American women wore lipstick—but only 96 percent brushed their teeth everyday. *Vogue*'s October 15, 1952, issue testifies to the reddened lip's universal appeal. The cover features a close-up of an unidentified woman's pillar-box-red mouth. The face, reads the copy, "might belong to any American woman. For lipstick is her inevitable signature."

Just a couple of months later, Revlon's Fire and Ice lipstick hit the market with one of the decade's best remembered ad campaigns. The two-page ad featured the ravenhaired model Dorian Leigh in a tight, silver-sequined sheath dress and a voluminous scarlet wrap. "Are you made for Fire and Ice?" it demanded. The copy included a coy "test" that was supposed to determine the answer to that question. "Have you ever danced with your shoes off? Do you sometimes feel that other women resent you? Do you close you're eyes when you're kissed?" The questions were calculated to make every woman who read them want to answer yes, because doing so would make her feel sexy, adventurous, and just a wee bit dangerous—a real Fire and Ice girl. The ads were hailed as brilliant, and the color became Revlon's top shade. (In fact, it still sells respectably today.)

What made this ad different from preceding ones was its single-minded focus on the woman wearing the lipstick. There was no man in sight, and no romance was alluded to. Instead, the ad suggested that applying lipstick was something a woman did for her own pleasure and gratification. This is certainly true—women wear lipstick to please themselves, not men, who tend to complain that it tastes funny. This recognition of the obvious represented a sea-change in cosmetics advertising and established a theme that is still used today. "Indulge yourself with something sweet," urges a recent ad for Revlon's Super Lustrous Lipstick. If kissable lips are mentioned in today's lipstick ads, it's to emphasize the long-lasting quality of the lip color.

By the early 1960s, fashionable women were shunning the bright shades of the postwar years for ingenue pinks and pallid oranges. Jacqueline Kennedy, a good decade younger than most political wives of the early 1960s, wore an orangey pink, while her older peers still wore tried-and-true red. The new emphasis on youth had the effect of making traditional lipsticks seem old-fashioned. Like high heels, another fashion made irrelevant by what Diana Vreeland termed the Youth Quake, lipstick is associated with grown-up, sophisticated women. A first lipstick was a milestone in a woman's life. By the mid-1960s, women weren't trying to look like adults, they were trying to look like children. They grew their hair long, wore thigh-skimming smock dresses and flat-heeled Mary Janes, and made up their eyes to look enormous and Bambilike. As the Youth Quake picked up speed, lipstick paled into white. Photos of mothers and daughters taken at the time show a color-themed gender gap, with older women sporting the precisely filled-in lips of the 1950s and younger ones looking like they don't have mouths at all, just the saucer eyes of children in black velvet paintings. In magazines, models were shown with flowers painted on their faces, or in full body makeup. Lipsticks were gold or glittery purple—fantasy, not sexual attraction was the goal.

The late '60s marked a time of shifting attitudes toward beauty. Feminists charged that women were held up to impossible standards when it came to their appearances, standards that took precedence over intelligence and talent. In 1968, protesters crowned a sheep Miss America, a stunt that drew a lot of media coverage. (This was the same protest at which a barrel full of objects that represented some of the rigid cultural ideals that women were held up to was burned. The bra in the barrel gave rise to the legend of bra-burning radical feminists.) Young women who supported the women's movement stopped wearing cosmetics as a way of expressing their solidarity. They wanted to look like themselves rather than some cosmetics manufacturer's ideal woman.

The industry responded by shifting the focus of its ads. Instead of referencing romance and glamour, advertisements played into the growing preoccupation with all things natural (health, beauty, food) by touting a lipstick's organic ingredients or the honey-and-wheatgerm base of a shampoo. Though there were some exceptions—notably adherents of the London-based Biba look of decadent maroon lips, raccoon eyes, and droopy 1930s-style fashions—most young women, if they were at all interested in makeup, wanted to look as though they weren't wearing any. "When people say to me, 'Why don't you use any makeup? You work for a cosmetics house?' I know I've been successful. I'm usually wearing about twelve products," one woman bragged to *Vogue* in 1976. An Avon ad from the same year boasted that its new Candid line "looks so real, feels so comfortable, it can only be called Candid." This was the era of lip gloss, a lighter, less dramatic form of lip coloring. Many glosses, such as Bonne Bell's popular flavored Lip Smackers, were completely sheer, providing only a high beam shine.

As in Victorian times, the "false face" was feared, though for different reasons and by different groups. In the nineteenth century, it was usually younger women who dared to sneak on a bit of lip tint while their elders shunned any hint of artifice. In the '70s, older women kept on making up the way they had since the '50s, complete with bright lipstick, and couldn't understand why young women didn't care enough about their looks to perm their hair or color their lips.

Working women were hesitant to wear too much makeup because pundits such as John T. Molloy, the best-selling author of *The Woman's Dress for Success Book*, discouraged it on the premise that a woman trying to break into a man's world should downplay her femininity. This brand of feminism didn't make it through the 1980s, when pop icons such as Madonna preached girl power through femininity. At the same time, the robust economy turned personal display into a competition, with first prize going to the most ostentatiously groomed and gowned. The powerful women of that decade, including cosmetics queen Georgette Mosbacher and First Lady Nancy Reagan, who matched her lips to her Reagan-red frocks, flaunted full faces of makeup along with their Scaasi dresses and Judith Leiber minaudières. On television, this look was epitomized by the claw-bearing vixens of *Dynasty*, for whom glamour was a weapon and fuchsia lips standard breakfast-table attire. In September 1985, *Vogue* explained the new trend to its readers: "And nowhere, this fall, is there more impact than from makeup: more color, brighter color—red lips, flashes of color on the eye. That's the switch for the season: you need that bit more."

By 1993, the year grunge hit fashion, the glamazons of

the 1980s looked overdone and tacky. Pale and wan was in, shoulder pads and vermilion lips were out. But fashion is famously fickle, and the aggressively unpretty waif look didn't last. Red lips came back with a roar in 1997, the same year the stiletto heel made a reappearance. Fashion had latched onto a tougher kind of sexuality.

Though there have been a few attempts to revive full-on '80s makeup, most notably on the catwalk, for the most part the late 1990s and early 2000s have been more subdued. "Pretty and natural" is the most common refrain you'll hear from the makeup artists who are quoted endlessly in the beauty sections—a wistfully innocent name for pages full of makeup advice—of women's magazines. The tricks of the trade have changed since the 1970s, of course. Stains, liquids that give lips a sheer but intense and long-lasting wash of color, are one new choice for women who want to achieve what the June 2002 issue of *Allure* calls "looking like you, only better." Balms that offer just a hint of color are popular, and lip gloss (along with denim, Carlos Falchi bags, and the trouser suit) has been resurrected from its '70s grave. And, in a latter-day twist on the wheat-germ-and-honey cosmetics of the era, Tony and Tina, a small cosmetics company based in New York, puts St. John's wort, the herb billed as the natural Prozac, in its lipsticks.

However, the same month that *Allure* was instructing its readers on how to look like modestly improved versions of themselves, *Harper's Bazaar* declared, "Classic red lips are always in style." Amen to that. Lipstick, I'm happy to say, isn't going anywhere. Makeup fads come and go, but lipstick is a perennial. The reason lies in the intense feminine associations this enigmatic cosmetic arouses. Lipstick is femininity in a tube, packaged, color-coded, and yours for as little as ninety-nine cents. As such, its lure is irresistible—even women who rarely wear it find themselves mesmerized by drugstore lipstick displays. Applying lipstick is an all-around sensual experience, from the satisfying instant spent contemplating the color to the intimate caress of gliding it along your lips. Its scent evokes memories as powerful as the taste of Proust's madeleine (in fact, Editions de Parfums Frédéric Malle recently created a fragrance called Lipstick Rose, the scent of which is supposed to evoke a woman who is "half Gilda, half Silvana Mangano, inspiring to everyone at one time or another"), while a lipstick color can recall an entire era—think of Erwin Blumenfeld's famous *Vogue* cover of 1950, which showed nothing but Jean Patchett's doe eye and the immaculate rose red arc of her mouth. With that kind of power behind it, who would willingly give up the tube?

Sneakers

There is a spiritual virtue and value that are implied by shoes like that. You can't slink like you can in a stiletto, so it represents a new form of femininity. It implies a new kind of strength.

—Anne Hollander

TRAVELING WITH OUR PARENTS ON A TRIP TO EUROPE when we were small, my sister and I invented a game to amuse ourselves during afternoons spent inspecting churches and touring museums: We would try to figure out where our fellow tourists were from. The rule was that we had to guess based on visual clues, which were then confirmed by standing close enough to the group in question to hear what language they were speaking. Though we became quite good at this game, we still made mistakes. Hearty-looking shorts wearers, for example, were quite often German—except when they turned out to be Australian. And the deeply tanned smokers could be either Italian or Brazilian—and sometimes even French. We rarely had trouble spotting Americans, though, because they had two main identifying characteristics: One, they were extremely friendly. And two, no matter their age or gender, they were shod in sneakers.

This game would be much more difficult to play today, because nationality is no longer quite so visible. Once upon a time, Americans were looked down upon for dressing like oversized children, in jeans, sweatshirts, and sneakers. As inhabitants of the global village, we all dress like Americans: Get on an international flight and your fellow passengers will most likely be wearing exactly that combination. You would have to check their passports to determine their country of origin.

A generation ago, sneakers would never have been listed along with the little black dress and the string of pearls as an iconic component of a woman's wardrobe. The redoubtable Mme. Geneviève Antoine-Dariaux, whose 1964 tome, *Elegance*, is referred to constantly in these pages, never mentions sneakers; I shudder to think what she would have to say about women pairing them with suits. Ellen Melinkoff, who describes less rarified circles than Mme. Antoine-Dariaux did, remembers that in the early '60s in the United States, high school girls wore white sneakers, which they paired with stockings. "The stockings were usually a shade or two darker than skin tone and looked swarthy against the white of the sneakers. Stockings and sneakers were never the height of fashion. They never made *Vogue* or *Women's Wear Daily*, but that's what everyone wore."

However, by 1998 no less a fashion authority than *Harper's Bazaar* quoted designer Daryl Kerrigan as saying, "The sneaker has become part of the library of necessary items for most women's wardrobes." In that same issue, editor-in-chief Liz Tilberis noted, "My editors all seem to be running around in sneakers. Wearing sneakers has become not just acceptable but a fashion statement."

What's unusual about Tilberis's observation is not that her fashionista editors were wearing a sports-inspired trend. While fashion and potentially sweaty exercise may sound like mutually exclusive pursuits, sports, particularly high-status ones such as golf and sailing, have long had an impact on what we wear. Ralph Lauren, for one, has built a lucrative empire on the notion that people who have never mounted a horse want to look as if they spend every weekend riding to the hounds. Looking like an athlete is a goal sanctioned by fashion because it implies that one has the time and money to devote to an activity that has nothing to do with making a living.

Instead, what is really surprising about the *Bazaar* staff flaunting sneakers is that they are wearing shoes that are not only stylish, but practical and comfortable—qualities that are generally considered fashion liabilities. Fashion is built on exclusivity, and nothing is more exclusive than impractical shoes. If you have to walk any distance, the very worst thing you can wear is high heels. Rather than torture your feet, you end up spending money on a cab. Sneakers, on the other hand, make walking a cheap pleasure.

For most of the twentieth century, women wore uncomfortable shoes as a matter of course. Gnarled toes and bunions were the price of femininity—partly because there were no other options. I once complimented my husband's septuagenarian grandmother on her snazzy white sneakers, a recent addition to her wardrobe. She grabbed my arm and said, with the excitement of a recent convert, "These are the most comfortable shoes I've ever worn!" My mother, a generation younger, still winces when she remembers the pointy-toed pumps of the early 1960s. If I wear uncomfortable shoes, it's with the knowledge that I can, if I decide to, kick them off and slouch around in sneakers.

In some ways, at least, we've come a long way, baby.

The sneaker is the most modern of the items in this book. Like jeans, its origins date to the nineteenth century. But it wasn't until the 1970s that sneakers were considered anything other than shoes to wear while you played sports, and well into the 1990s before they were worn by the fashion elite. Sneakers are nominally still spoils-oriented—for example, basketball stars are prominently featured in advertising, and manufacturers continue to insist that their shoes are designed for serious athletes. However, Nike changes the designs of its uppers every six months, a move that has nothing to do with running faster or jumping farther. It does, however, have everything to do with creating demand. Today, the real purpose of the sneaker is to indicate one's taste and style allegiances. The sneaker is no longer a mere shoe, it is a lifestyle product.

It is this latest reincarnation that has pushed the sneaker into fashion's front ranks. As Tom Vanderbilt, the author of *The Sneaker Book*, puts it, "The sneaker is to other shoes as sport-utility vehicles are to other cars: large, loaded with impressive but rarely used options, a statement less of need than of desire."

I have several pairs of sneakers, none of which I really need. I don't run or play tennis or even belong to a gym. In fact, all my sneakers were chosen for their looks, the same way I pick all my other shoes. The blue suede Adidas Gazelles I bought because they have an agreeably low-key, old-school vibe—and they look good with all shades of denim. The orange and red New Balances were selected because they contrast nicely with tailored black trousers. And the white Converse All Star low-cuts are like a plain white T-shirt: classic, clean-cut but not boring, and always reliable. In the ranks of the sneaker savvy, I am close to the bottom, though not quite bringing up the rear. I would no more wear aesthetically questionable sneakers than I would acid-wash jeans—but I love other kinds of shoes too much to devote myself to tracking down the perfect pair, especially since that pair changes every month. Nor can I bring myself to call them trainers—Brit-speak for sneaker—as many North American sneaker lovers do, in homage to the lofty position the sneaker occupies in British style.

The genesis of the sneaker-as-fashion-accessory in North America dates to 1995, and the release of the Nike Air Max with the color-graduated upper. I suspect that this sneaker was adopted by fashionistas as part of the first wave of the ugly shoe trend of the mid-1990s. This trend arose as a way of winnowing the true fashionistas from the wannabe fashionistas, a distinction that became necessary in the wake of the post-Prada, post-Gucci fashion obsession that gripped consumers at that time. The media-driven rise of these two brands transformed fashion from the concern of a select few to a highly visible game of grab as much as you can. Suddenly, Prada knapsacks and Gucci loafers seemed as common as Levi's and sweatshirts. Fashion labels floated IPOs, celebrities became front-row fixtures at runway shows, and *In Style* blossomed into a best-selling magazine. Fashion began to look like a branch of the entertainment industry. To preserve their hauteur, style pundits began to wear fashions that, to the average eye, looked downright hideous: Shoes with clunky heels and ungainly proportions were especially popular (see any Prada design from 1995 to 1999 for references). Sneakers, which had been snubbed by the stylish for so long, were another natural choice. The Air Max came along just in time.

When the original model sold out in the shops, its street price climbed to four digits. The January 1997 version of the Air Max, which was made of futuristic looking silver mesh, sent consumers into an even more rabid frenzy. *Wallpaper*, the lifestyle and travel magazine that shaped an entire generation's aesthetic, advised its readers to keep an unworn pair on hand because their value was sure to multiply. Once the style sold out, that's exactly what happened, sending people like Frank DeCaro, a style reporter for *The New York Times*, into a panic. DeCaro wrote a piece about his months-long search for the elusive Air Max that begins, "When you have spent countless hours calling Kissimmee, Fla., Dry Ridge, Ky., and Pigeon Forge, Tenn., in search of silver shoes, you are most definitely a fashion obsessive."

The metallic Air Max also appeared in *Harper's Bazaar* and

Vogue, and was spotted on such trendsetters as Gwen Stefani of No Doubt and Madonna. Certain sneakers had been hip before, but the popularity of the Air Max was unprecedented. It catapulted the athletic shoe into the foreground of style. In fact, the Air Max was so popular that it inspired its very own backlash: In 1998, the cutting-edge British magazine *The Face* declared that anyone who wore this sneaker "was in league with the devil." The Air Max had become too mainstream, and that's a dirty word to sneaker fanatics.

Without the ingenuity of a man named Charles Goodyear, the brouhaha over the Air Max could never have been. Goodyear was an American hardware salesman and inventor who, in 1836, received a patent for vulcanizing rubber, a process which rendered raw sap firm and stable enough to be used for shoe soles. Rubber-soled shoes had existed before Goodyear's discovery, but they were notoriously unreliable. Unvulcanized rubber has the consistency of chewing gum—it will melt in hot weather and harden and crack when the temperature drops. Goodyear's invention needed a lot of fine-tuning—he didn't perfect it until 1868—but shoe manufacturers seized on the new concept right away. By 1870, "sneaks" were widely known in the United States as rubber-soled shoes with canvas uppers. And by the turn of the twentieth century, mass-market retailers such as Sears sold sneaks for sixty cents a pair.

The earliest known reference to an athletic shoe dates to 1517, when a visitor to the English court noted that Henry VIII had a pair of "shooys with feltys, to play in at Tennys." By the nineteenth century, Henry's primitive sneakers had evolved into white, rubber-soled "croquet sandals," which were worn for such genteel sports as lawn tennis, cricket, and, of course, croquet.

This high-falutin' image began to change early in the twentieth century. Organizations such as the YMCA promoted the idea of a healthy mind in a healthy body to the working classes, and participation in sports—for boys, at least—was encouraged by schools and civic organizations. In 1916, the U.S. Rubber Co. introduced Keds—the name is a combination of "kids" and "ped," Latin for foot—a sneaker aimed specifically at children. The following year, the Converse Rubber Co. produced the first All Star sneaker, a basketball shoe that quickly became a favorite of American boys. Six years later, the company displayed a prescient grasp of the power of celebrity endorsement when it signed up pro player Chuck Taylor to be the All Star's spokesmodel. Unlike today's well-compensated stars, however, Taylor was paid a pittance—and he actually traveled the country hosting basketball clinics and hawking sneakers.

Despite the popularity of sneakers, mothers worried that the flimsy canvas uppers didn't provide the support of sturdy brown oxfords, and schools didn't allow students to wear them to class. Sneakers were strictly for play. Among adults, sneakers were not considered appropriate attire anywhere other than the tennis court. In 1920, when the trend-setting Prince of Wales wore tennis shoes on his American tour, his informality was considered quite shocking. Nevertheless, the pairing of tennis shoes with street clothes was a popular affectation with young men throughout the '20s. For years afterward, the appearance in a film of a grown-up character wearing tennis shoes with street clothes signaled a reckless disregard for rules, a refusal to accept adult responsibilities. In 1962's *West Side Story*, rival gangs the Jets and the Sharks wear sneakers, while the adults wear conventional leather shoes. And in *All the President's Men* (1976), Dustin Hoffman, playing the whistle-blowing reporter Carl Bernstein, wears Adidas Gazelles in the newsroom. His patrician editor, portrayed by Jason Robards, wears wingtips. Real-life examples of the sneaker wearer as antiestablishment heroes include James Dean, who was often photographed wearing Jack Purcell sneakers, Andy Warhol, who gadded about in tattered Keds, and Woody Allen, who in the 1970s accessorized his tuxedo with red Converse high-tops.

It was in the 1960s, when dress codes relaxed and the first massive wave of baby boomers became teenagers, that sneakers became socially acceptable. According to Tom Vanderbilt, sales of sneakers in the United States went from 35 million pairs in 1952 to 150 million pairs in 1962. In response, sneaker manufacturers began to expand their offerings. Converse, after years of limited colors, introduced seven new shades in 1966. But for the most part, athleticism, not image, was what sneakers were associated with. A potential customer might be interested to know that a star athlete wore a particular sneaker, but this didn't arouse any desire to emulate that athlete's style.

That changed in 1968, when, for the first time, the Olympics were televised live. Struck by the prospect of millions of viewers tuning in and seeing their logos, Adidas and Puma, which were run by rival brothers, became engaged in an intense contest to get athletes into their gear, going so far as to stuff hundred-dollar bills into athletes' sneakers. Paying athletes to wear a brand wasn't new, but the '68 games increased the stakes considerably. In the end, the Adidas trefoil dominated in Mexico City, appearing not just on sneakers, but on equipment bags, T-shirts, and tracksuits. Adidas was established as a cool brand, a reputation the company rode well into the next decade. As a kindergartner in the mid-'70s, I remember that all the older boys carried their books in Adidas bags.

But Puma didn't lose out entirely. Among the athletes who wore Puma were the American Black Power runners Thomas Smith and Lee Evans. Smith and Evans were stripped of their medals after giving the Black Power salute on the podium, but their gesture gave Puma an aura of authenticity that resonated with African Americans. Puma followed this up in 1974 by becoming the first company to create a signature sneaker for a basketball player. Known as the Clyde, it was made for New York Knick Walt Frazier (he was nicknamed Clyde because of his penchant for wide-brimmed hats like the ones worn by Warren Beatty in *Bonnie and Clyde*). These events gave Puma an edge with young black consumers that was later reflected in the nascent hip-hop culture of the late 1970s and early 1980s, when wearing Pumas became an important fashion statement. Jamel Shabazz's book chronicling those early years, *Back in the Days*, is full of photos of B-boys wearing giant, heavy-framed glasses and immaculate suede Clydes (to be fair, many wear Adidas Gazelles, but the Clydes look so much cooler).

The 1970s set the stage for the cultural development that would propel the sneaker into fashion: the fitness revolution.

The baby boomers who in the 1960s had loudly proclaimed that you couldn't trust anyone over thirty were now facing that very age themselves. They were determined to hang on to their youth and looked to exercise as a way of preserving that elusive quality. As a result, sports were no longer something to be endured in gym class and then forgotten—being a jock was hip.

Partly through the media's coverage of telegenic players such as Chris Evert and Vitas Gerulaitis, tennis, which had formerly been associated with the gin-and-tonic set, was reinvented as a sport for hip young urbanites. In 1977's *Annie Hall,* for example, Woody Allen and Diane Keaton first meet on the tennis court of a Manhattan gym. But the most popular sport of the decade was running, and sneaker companies aimed themselves directly at the huge number of joggers. One of the most successful at capturing their attention was Nike.

Today, Nike is a behemoth. But its beginnings were quite humble. The company was launched in 1972, when Bill Bowerman, a running coach at the University of Oregon, showed Phil Knight, the founder of a modest sneaker company called Blue Ribbon Sports, a piece of rubber he had put in his waffle iron. The two glued the gridmarked rubber onto one of Knight's uppers, found that it made the sneaker lighter and stronger, and an empire was born. The shoe, known as the Nike, was so successful that the company was renamed in its honor. Within a year, the newly christened Nike was calling itself "the shoe for the '70s."

Nike's success lay in the company's intuitive grasp of the boomer mentality. In Donald Katz's *Just Do It: The Nike Spirit in the Corporate World,* a book that chronicles Nike's corporate culture, a marketer explains that Nike recognized early on that this youth-obsessed generation was at odds with its own mortality. Boomers didn't want to age and embraced various physical and spiritual schemes—health food, Eastern philosophies, jogging—to keep signs of decay from encroaching. (Significantly, one of the definitive boomer films, 1983's *The Big Chill*, features a character who made a fortune selling sneakers.) By being proactive, boomers seemed to think that they could hang on to youth indefinitely. Nike ads, which culminated in tough-love tag lines such as "there is no finish line," played right into that conceit.

Those who played sports wanted to advertise the fact, while those who didn't wanted to look as if they did, in fact, know what was meant by an endorphin high. In 1980, the fashion designer Norma Kamali capitalized on this trend by designing a collection built around gray cotton fleece, a fabric more commonly associated with gym class than with high style. Kamali's designs included details such as peplums and shoulder pads, but for the most part, the clothes resembled workout gear. Women accessorized Kamali's designs with white Keds and ankle socks, as though they were on their way to an aerobics class rather than the office.

Among urban adults, physical perfection was as desirable as an impressive stock portfolio. Joining a health club became a routine part of life. Consumers snapped up Jane Fonda's workout tapes, watched Olivia Newton John get "Physical" in a pastel leotard on MTV, and cut open the necklines of their sweatshirts in homage to Jennifer Beals's character in *Flashdance*. When a transit strike forced New Yorkers to walk to work in 1980, women adapted by wearing their Reebok aerobics sneakers with their business suits for the trek to the office, changing into loafers or slingbacks only once they reached their desks. In the beginning, this pairing was treated as an exciting new fad—*Vogue* even named walking to work in sneakers the hot new form of exercise. But within a couple of years, it had become associated with a distinctly lower-class aesthetic. In the 1988 film *Working Girl*, for example, Melanie Griffith and her fellow outer-borough secretaries are seen taking the Staten Island ferry to work, their nylon-covered legs descending from bright, knee-baring skirts into ankle socks and puffy white sneakers—a direct contrast to the upwardly mobile yuppies epitomized by Sigourney Weaver, who strides off the elevator in neat pumps and a dark suit.

Another factor that kept sneakers popular was basketball, a sport that emerged as the glamour game of the 1980s. Sneaker companies had been making endorsement deals with NBA players since the 1970s, but it wasn't until 1984, when Nike signed Michael Jordan of the Chicago Bulls, for a then astounding $2.5 million, that the possibilities for using a player's personality to sell shoes was fully realized. Jordan's charisma was such that Air Jordans took in $130 million for Nike the first year they were sold. Even more significantly, they raised the profile of basketball shoes to the point that every sneaker manufacturer was scrambling to sign an NBA player.

The growing interest in basketball coincided with the rise of hip-hop, a subculture that took sneaker fetishism to new extremes. If a particular sneaker was favored by a well-known rapper, sales of that model would escalate. In 1986, Run-D.M.C. released a song called "My Adidas," about their preferred kicks. When they performed the song in concert, fans would wave their Adidas over their heads. The company eventually signed the group to an endorsement deal, thus implicitly acknowledging that sneakers had moved away from their athletic roots and closer to their new role as lifestyle emblems. When Jam Master Jay, Run-D.M.C.'s DJ, was shot and killed in a New York City recording studio in October 2002, fans piled their Adidas outside the building in an impromptu shrine.

Though most hip-hop CDs—and most sneakers—were sold to white kids in the suburbs, black urban teenagers provided the standard on which both industries modeled their product. For sneaker manufacturers, this involved visiting playgrounds in neighborhoods such as Harlem or East L.A. with bags of shoes for kids to look at, a practice known as "bro'ing," as in, "Hey, bro, what do you think of this sneaker?". Designs that didn't win approval from inner-city teenagers were reconfigured or dropped altogether. Sneaker advertising began to reflect the violent aesthetic of the "thug life"; one ad for LA Gear even showed basketball player Michael Johnson holding a machine gun.

In the minds of many white, middle- and upper-class Americans, sneakers were associated with drugs, gangs, and violence, an assumption Tom Wolfe satirized in his 1987 novel *The Bonfire of the Vanities*. Sneaker references pop up regularly in Wolfe's tale of racial tension and class animosity set in a decaying New York City. One character, an assistant district attorney, wears Nike sneakers for the subway ride to and from work because they are "camouflage. On the subway in the Bronx, a pair of Johnston & Murphy leather business shoes labeled you as a prime target right off the bat. It was like wearing a sign around your neck saying ROB ME."

In reality, wearing sneakers could *cause* you to become the victim of a mugging. By 1990, the media was regularly reporting that kids were being robbed for their sneakers (Nike's Air Jordans, which retailed for more than $100, were the most popular target). Sneakers came to be at the center of a national debate about violence and an increasingly materialistic culture. Prominent African Americans, including the Rev. Jesse Jackson, spoke out against companies—particularly Nike, which commanded 40 percent of the market—that advertised increasingly expensive shoes to poor, inner-city kids.

Nike's image suffered even more a few years later, when stories began to surface about how little the company paid its mostly female employees in Asia. By the late-'90s Nike's market dominance was no longer the formidable force it once was. As a reaction against the supremely flashy, money-oriented culture of the 1980s and early 1990s, consumers began to favor more low-tech styles. "High tech is burned out," declared Puma creative director Antonio Bertone in the April 1998 issue of *Harper's Bazaar.* In its place, consumers were seeking out low-tech designs from the 1970s and the classic styles offered by Tretorn, Converse, and Spring Court, companies whose shoes had changed very little since their introduction. Camper, a Spanish company, started a worldwide trend with its 1950s bowling styles.

In the fashion world, sneakers with a look of geek chic had particular cachet. New Balance, a British company that had never had any pretensions to style, proved a surprise hit in the fall of 1997, when the designer Jean Colonna showed them on his runway. A few months later, the New Balance trend was being cited in mainstream publications. "For a sneaker that was once looked upon by the fashion conscious as the Volvo of running shoes, New Balance is making big strides. Drab, gray-on-gray New Balances are suddenly emblems of low-profile, retro coolness," reported *The New York Times* in April 1998. An important factor in the sudden trendiness of the New Balance was the rarity of certain colors. The red sneakers shown by Colonna, for example, were sold only in the United Kingdom. Sporting red New Balances in New York signified that the wearer was a savvy, well-traveled trendsetter, the kind of person who knew where to find the best kicks in London, the hippest bar in the 11th arrondisement, the most ironic T-shirt in Tokyo. Acquiring obscure sneakers soon became its own competitive sport.

Fashionistas paired their hard-to-find styles with high-end designs such as Balenciaga trousers and Fendi handbags. They even wore them with suits, like the Wall Streeters of the early 1980s. But this time around, the sneakers weren't puffy white eyesores to be stowed in a desk drawer during working hours. In the mid- and late '90s, women wore their sleek sky blue New Balances or minimalist black-and-gray Pumas to work and kept them on all day. It was a look with a definitive message. A woman in a Helmut Lang suit and firecracker red New Balances was signifying that she was hip, busy, smart, and competitive—not someone to be taken lightly. By embracing such a utilitarian shoe, women weren't rejecting feminine display, as they did when they donned navy blue suits in the late 1970s, but rather redefining it. It is now acceptable to wear sneakers with low-cut top and tight pants; many young women alternate between the highest of heels and the brightest of athletic shoes and see nothing incongruous about the contrast. Designer Stella McCartney, whose sweet and tarty style has been enormously influential on young women, frequently appears in public in sneakers. In 1999, British *Vogue* writer Christa D'Souza described one of McCartney's signature ensembles: "She herself is wearing a flowery Chloé dress from a past season, with the arms ripped off so the edges are fraying, no bra, a pair of grey trousers, and Adidas Stan Smith sneakers. All of which is perfectly offset by a deep freckly tan . . . and a huge diamond bracelet." Girly prints, broken-in kicks, and an eye-catching jewel: Of such juxtapositions is modern style born.

By the spring of 1998, even Parisiennes, who had once looked down on American women because of their penchant for mixing athletic shoes with business clothes, got hip to the sneaker's new image. "All of a sudden, French women who have never been shod in anything more décontracté than Inès de la Fressange moccasins are turning up in canvas Guess shoes, suede Pumas, old-school Adidas, even Skechers, the official footgear of the global skate-rat fraternity," reported Guy Trebay in *The New York Times Magazine* that April. Trebay went on to describe the new sneaker put out by Hermès, the French luxury goods brand best known for its $5000-saddle-bag inspired purses. Known as the Quick, the Hermès sneaker was available in white, black, gold, or natural leather, looked vaguely orthopedic, and retailed for a steep $525. Quick was sold out in Paris, Trebay noted, and had a three-month waiting list in New York.

Hermès was not the only high-fashion company to jump on the sneaker train—the fashion industry will turn whatever it needs to survive into a luxury item. In a move comparable to the designer jean trend of the mid-'70s, Gucci, Prada, and Chanel all debuted athletic shoes, many of which sold for more than four hundred dollars. Other designers chose to collaborate with existing sneaker manufacturers: Jil Sander worked with Puma, while Yohji Yamamoto has paired up with Adidas. These shoes sell well among the fashion conscious who want the status of a name without the continent-hopping required to track down only-in-Japan rarities.

At less lofty price points were companies such as Skechers, Acupuncture, and Royal Elastics, style-minded upstarts in a market that had always stressed its commitment to athletic achievement. These new brands made no such claims; instead, their shoes unabashedly glorified form over function. Acupuncture's controversial ads made no reference to sports at all. Instead, they used kinky situations to establish the London-based company's dark, rebellious image. In one, a couple gets sexual satisfaction from beating a fellow foot fetishist to death; another depicts a man masturbating with his sneaker. The ads provided an interesting comment on the increasing fetishization of sneakers.

Skechers landed an appearance in the 2002 film *About a Boy*, starring Hugh Grant. In the film, Grant befriends an awkward twelve-year-old. In an attempt to make the boy appear cooler to the loutish bullies who torment him, Grant takes him shopping for Skechers sneakers. The plan works all too well: The sneakers are stolen right off his feet by his covetous peers. The theft suggests that Skechers are so cool that even outcasts can become the object of envy if they wear them. But among the sneaker elite, Skechers are too ubiquitous to be desirable. For the upper-echelon sneaker aficionado, the main joy in a shoe is its exclusivity. These types shop at boutiques such as Alife Rivington Club, a shop on the Lower East Side of Manhattan that has a doorbell but no sign, and carries sneakers not available anywhere else in North America (and therefore unlikely to be seen on the feet of suburban dilettantes). Entire Web sites are devoted to tracking down rare sneaker styles.

Even mainstream companies such as Nike and Reebok are using elements of underground hipness to sell their product. As reported on the Worth Global Style Network (WGSN) in July 2002, instead of awarding multimillion-dollar contracts to NBA stars, these brands are searching out unknown street players "with fancy ball-handling techniques and an 'urban' image," and signing them for far less money. WGSN quoted a *Wall Street Journal* article: "Savvy consumers . . . are increasingly resistant to ads for shoes named after National Basketball Association players."

What consumers demand more than any other quality in their purchases right now is authenticity, and that's not something that can be faked. Post-Enron, corporate executives have merged into one another in the mind of the public as overprivileged villains—and what are billion-dollar basketball players if not the executives of the sports world? In the current economic climate, anything corporate smacks of opportunism. Street players, who compete for the love of the game rather than six-figure salaries, seem far more sympathetic to today's sneaker lovers than anyone in the NBA. In a parallel development, the bands that are getting the most play right now are playing three-chord, DIY rock, and they—and their fans—are wearing ratty T-shirts and low-cut Converses. In a piece about this new bohemia in *The New York Times*, a reporter noted that no one in this crowd "would be caught . . . wearing Prada sneakers." They'd be far more likely to be sporting the newly popular ProKeds, a line that Keds introduced in the 1940s and that is now enjoying a renaissance among the urban hip, or perhaps Puma's Top Winner Thrift model, each pair of which is made from a single vintage garment (the latter would be less likely, as only 510 pairs of these were produced).

For the moment, at least, old school and low-key are in. This will change, of course. The economy will improve, unbridled capitalism will look good again, and sneaker styles will go high-tech. But for now, I'm enjoying this Luddite footwear moment. It seems truer to the indie vibe that sneakers have traditionally been associated with than the silver-toned excesses of the early 1990s. Moreover, I've already got a pair of low-cut Cons in my closet. And every time I wear them, I get compliments. What more could a shoe lover want out of her sneakers?

Conclusion

Honoré de Balzac once observed that those who see only fashion in fashion are fools. I've never doubted this, but after researching and writing *The Classic Ten,* I have an even deeper appreciation for the truth—so simple on the surface!—of Balzac's remark. Fashion, no matter how frivolous it may appear, is never just about covering the body. We wear our clothes right next to our skin; they're intensely personal, revealing both how we see ourselves and how we'd like to be seen. Next time you're in a public place, look around at what people are wearing. Every item of clothing you see was chosen over a multitude of others—its owner walked into a shop and selected it for a reason.

If you do go through with this exercise, my guess is that the clothes you'll spot more than any others are the ones discussed in this book. They are part of fashion, as opposed to Fashion (although sometimes they cross over into capital-F territory, as when a designer decides that a season is all about the white shirt). The former is what people really wear; the latter is what is shown on the runways and photographed for glossy magazines. Though not as heavily promoted as some of the more transitory trends, the histories and the subleties of small-f fashion are compelling; the ten items described in this book hold as many secrets and memories as Proust's madeleine. The histories of the LBD, the trench coat, high heels, and the rest, steeped as they are in such basic human instincts as the need to feel sexually attractive and the desire for power, have ensured these items a berth in countless closets, not to mention a well-earned place in cultural history. It has also made them an awful lot of fun to write about and, I hope, to read about.

Selected Bibliography

Batterberry, Michael and Ariane. *Fashion: The Mirror of History.* London: Greenwich House, 1982.

Brown, Christine. "Cashmere's Cachet: How Chinese Economic Liberation Helped Make Cashmere Sweaters More Affordable in the U. S." *Forbes,* April 10, 1995.

Corson, Richard. *Fashions in Makeup: From Ancient to Modern Times.* London: Peter Owen Books, 1972.

Dariaux, Gabrielle. *Elegance.* Garden City, N.Y.: Doubleday, 1964.

DeCaro, Frank. "Style Over Substance: Tied Up in Knots in the Race for a Shoe." *The New York Times Magazine,* March 29, 1998.

Downey, Lynn, Jill Lynch, and Kathleen McDonough. *This Is a Pair of Levi's Jeans.* San Francisco: Levi Strauss & Co. Publishing, 1995.

Edelman, Amy Holdman. *The Little Black Dress.* New York: Simon & Schuster, 1997.

Edwards, Owen. "Bogey Nights." *GQ,* April, 2002.

Etcoff, Nancy. *Survival of the Prettiest.* New York: Anchor Books, 2000.

Finlayson, Iain. *Denim: An American Legend.* New York: Fireside, 1990.

Fogarty, Anne. *Wife Dressing.* New York: Julian Messner, 1959.

Fowler, Marian. *The Way She Looks Tonight*. New York: St. Martin's Press, 1996.

Fraser, Kennedy. *The Fashionable Mind, Reflections on Fashion, 1970–1981*. Boston: David R. Godine, 1984.

Goldsmith, Barbara. *Little Gloria . . . Happy at Last*. New York: Dell, 1980.

Hirschberg, Lynn. "She Wears the Pants." *Harper's Bazaar,* April 2001.

Hollander, Anne. *Seeing Through Clothes.* New York: Avon, 1980.

———. *Sex and Suits: The Evolution of Modern Dress.* New York: Alfred A. Knopf, 1994.

———. *Feeding the Eye.* Berkeley: University of California Press, 2000.

Howell, Georgina. *In Vogue: Sixty Years of International Celebrities and Fashion from British Vogue.* New York: Schocken Books, 1976.

Iverson, Annemarie. "Ode to the White Shirt." *Harper's Bazaar,* June 1998.

Jackson, Jennifer. "Sneaker Chic." *Harper's Bazaar,* April 1998.

Jacobs, Laura. "Gowned for Glory." *Vanity Fair,* November 1998.

Landman, Neil H., Paula M. Mikkelson, Rüdiger Bieler, and Bennet Bronson. *Pearls: A Natural History*. New York: Harry N. Abrams, Inc., 2001.

Ludot, Didier. *The Little Black Dress: Vintage Treasure.* New York: Assouline, 2001.

Lurie, Alison. *The Language of Clothes.* New York: Owl Books, 2000.

Macy, Caitlin. "Meeting My Maker." *The New York Times Magazine,* August 20, 2002.

Madsen, Axel. *Chanel: A Woman of Her Own.* New York: Henry Holt and Co., 1991.

Magnuson, Ann. "Hell on Heels." *Allure,* September 1994.

Mead, Rebecca. "The Crisis in Cashmere." *The New Yorker,* February 1, 1999.

Melinkoff, Ellen. *What We Wore: An Offbeat Social History of Women's Clothing, 1950–1980.* New York: Quill, 1984.

Mendes, Valerie. *Dressed in Black.* London: V&A Publications, 1999.

Merriam, Eve. *Fig Leaf: The Business of Being in Fashion.* New York: J.B. Lippincott Company, 1960.

Molloy, John T. *The Women's Dress for Success Book.* New York: Warner Books, 1977.

Nicholson, Geoff. *Footsucker.* Woodstock, N.Y.: Overlook Press, 1996.

O'Keefe, Linda. *Shoes: A Celebration of Pumps, Sandals, Slippers & More.* New York: Workman Publishing, 1996.

Pallingston, Jessica. *Lipstick: A Celebration of the World's Favorite Cosmetic.* New York: St. Martin's Press, 1999.

Peiss, Kathy. *Hope in a Jar: The Making of America's Beauty Culture.* New York: Henry Holt and Co., 1998.

Pochna, Marie-France. *Christian Dior: The Man Who Made the World Look New.* New York: Arcade Publishing, 1996.

Ragas, Meg Cohen and Karen Kozlowski. *Read My Lips: A Cultural History of Lipstick.* San Francisco: Chronicle Books, 1998.

Reed, Julia. "Strung Out." *Vogue,* February 2001.

Rossi, William. *The Sex Life of the Foot and Shoe.* New York: Krieger Publishing Company, 1993.

Specter, Michael. "High Heel Heaven." *The New Yorker.* March 20, 2000.

Steele, Valerie. *Fetish: Fashion, Sex & Power.* New York: Oxford University Press, 1996.

———. *Fifty Years of Fashion: New Look to Now.* New Haven: Yale University Press, 1977.

———. *Paris Fashion: A Cultural History*. New York: Berg, 1998.

———. *Shoes: A Lexicon of Style.* New York: Rizzoli, 1999.

Steinhauer, Jennifer. "Walk Softly and Make a Big Statement." *The New York Times,* May 17, 1998.

Steinhauer, Jennifer and Constance C. R. White. "Women's New Relationship With Fashion." *The New York Times,* August 5, 1996.

———. "Fashion Relearns Its Darwin: Be Adaptable or Be Extinct." *The New York Times,* August 5, 1996.

Sykes, Plum. "Caught in Customs." *Vogue,* November 2002.

Tapert, Annette and Diana Edkins. *The Power of Style.* New York: Crown Publishers, 1994.

Trebay, Guy. "Sneaker Attack." *The New York Times Magazine,* April 26, 1998.

Van Meter, Jonathan. "Fast Fashion." *Vogue,* June 1990.

Vanderbilt, Tom. *The Sneaker Book.* New York: New Press, 1998.

Veblen, Thorstein. *The Theory of the Leisure Class.* New York: Penguin Books, 1994.